Training of the Infantry for Offensive Combat

By

Louis Loyzeau de Grandmaison

Legacy Books Press
Military Classics

Published by Legacy Books Press
RPO Princess, Box 21031
445 Princess Street
Kingston, Ontario, K7L 5P5
Canada

www.legacybookspress.com

This translation and edition first published in 2021 by Legacy Books Press
1

ISBN: 978-1-927537-51-0

First published as *Dressage de l'Infanterie en Vue du Combat Offensif*, Third Edition, in 1908 by Berger-Levrault & Cie.

Printed and bound in the United States of America and Canada.

This book is typeset in a Times New Roman 11-point font.

Table of Contents

Publisher's Note

Preface

The regulations set forth *principles*; it is up to the officers to find their own *methods* of application, which vary according to the conditions of the armament. The most recent wars have shown the extreme difficulty of the infantry attack; the methods of execution of this attack must therefore respond to new needs. However, not all officers are able to find the most satisfactory solutions right away.

Commander de Grandmaison, after having studied with the greatest care and a keen critical intelligence the most recent campaigns, sought the most suitable methods for the execution of the offensive. He renders the greatest service by sharing with his comrades the result of his reflections and his practical experience in commanding a battalion for several years.

Starting from the principle that only the offensive gives positive results, he aims especially, in the training, at the offensive combat. The teaching of the procedures of progression, on the most varied grounds, must thus take an important place in the whole of our preparation. During the whole duration of the forward movement, the direct action of the command on the engaged troop can no longer be felt and it is necessary that each combatant makes personal work; also the individual instruction of the man and his moral health take in the modern combat a capital importance. Although, theoretically, no one disputes it, these factors have not yet taken their rightful place in training practice. The result is that the training of the soldier, as the author so rightly says, must have an individualistic tendency and this training is done, as soon as the recruits arrive, in the middle of the campaign. One can only approve of this method.

Does this mean that combat is no longer conducted? The commander does not fall into this error. The role of the command tends more and more to "regulate the intensity of the fight on the different parts of the front" by the play of its reserves, according to the very terms of the decree on the service of armies in the field.

Individualism should not, however, make us lose sight of the need for cohesion; this, says the author, is the result of "the habit of acting collectively with a view to a common goal"; the training of the group consists of creating these habits, and always on varied terrain.

The offensive is the forward movement; fire has no other purpose than to enable the advance. When one considers the offensive by considering the action of the infantry alone, one comes up against such real difficulties that one tends to conclude that attacks are impossible, a depressing and false conclusion. Forward movement, in the zone of effective fire, becomes impossible if the assailant does not have fire superiority, established by the cessation or the harmlessness of the fire of the adversary who goes underground and no longer aims; this is certain. Now the superiority of fire, the infantry, alone, can rarely acquire it: the moving fractions cannot shoot, often they even mask the fire of the immobile fractions which could help them. The education of the group consists in attenuating this defect by inculcating in the very hearts of the cadres and the men the spirit of solidarity, a powerful moral factor which consists in always helping by its fire, as far as possible, the comrade who is going forward.

Nevertheless, the task of the infantry would still be too heavy; also the commander of Grandmaison expresses this very just thought that the problem of the offensive combat can be solved only by "the union of the arms." It was up to the artillery to achieve fire superiority. If this superiority was acquired frankly and could be maintained during the entire time of the attack and on the entire front under attack, the forward movement of the infantry would be nothing more than a marching maneuver. This is the goal to which the artilleryman must tend and which he would perhaps attain if the number of firearms and especially that of the projectiles at his disposal were unlimited. In most cases, this will not be the case. From then on, the artillery would act in bursts, and each burst would either allow the chain to make a leap forward, or allow the second line elements to join the chain, reinforce it or even push it forward. This burst, a real shield for the infantry, may not be able to be felt at the same time on the entire front under attack; it will then be applied successively to different zones and, in each of these zones, it will be the signal for a forward movement that it will cover. Such must be the link between the two weapons. Also we would like, to the so methodical exercises indicated by the author for the training of the infantry group, to add special exercises for the training of the mixed group, for the study of the linkage of the weapons. One would thus come to understand that if the power of current weapons makes it very difficult to make a poorly supported attack – and the Japanese as well as the Russians have supported their attacks very poorly – the material and moral effect of modern firearms facilitates, on the contrary, the offensive, even direct.

In the meantime, infantry officers will find in Major de Grandmaison's book, for the individual training of the troop, for the training of the group, for the deployment of the vanguards, etc., methods that depart from the routines that have been followed for too long and that have proven their worth through unquestionable results in maneuvers. They cannot read this booklet too much, meditate on it and draw precious information from it.

General H. Langlois

Foreword

There is a justified concern among infantry officers who are concerned with their profession. Are our training procedures appropriate on the one hand to the needs of modern combat and on the other hand to the necessities of short-term service? One is allowed to doubt it.

Today's combat requires a flexible infantry, very maneuverable and practically experienced in war firing. Short-term service requires that these results be obtained quickly.

We have already largely pruned our old regulations and given individual initiative a considerable share. This may not be enough. In order to obtain a more rapid and practical training of the troops, a few removed details are of little importance; it is the very spirit and – if I may say so – the mores of our training that must be modified.

The individual initiative generously assured is a fruitful conquest which we must not renounce; but, to bear fruit, this initiative must be based on a positive doctrine.

The study of offensive combat is the only solid basis that can be given to the instruction of the infantryman. The first part of this book is a short analysis of offensive combat as taught in recent wars. It is the common trunk on which all the branches of our instruction must be grafted.

The second part deals with the actual methods and their practical application.

In printing these notes, our aim is not to offer a guide to the lazy or to dig a new rut, but to provide instructors of good will with working materials tested by serious experience.

We would like, before anything else, to share with them the conviction that, in our profession, the most elevated, the most endearing and the most useful part of our task is instruction.

Part One: The Infantry in Offensive Combat

Chapter I – The Moral Forces

In this summary study of offensive combat strictly limited to the observations necessary to serve as a basis for our instruction, we will use the lessons beyond discussion imposed on us by the results of the British campaign in South Africa and what we already know of the Russian-Japanese war – referring, for the entire documentary part of the discussion, to the works published on the subject.

Moreover, we will not deal here with maneuver or combined battlefield tactics, but only with the form of infantry combat, the mechanism of the fight, one might say, if the word did not suggest an idea so contrary to the reality of things. For nothing in the world is further from mechanics.

Our ideas on the fight are vague and, with a bias, very optimistic. Even those who have fought do not always want to believe their memories, nor admit to their impressions. Risking one's life at every step for hours on end is not a game for the average man; also, whatever the adversary facing him, the man in combat has only one enemy: fear, and it is the one he talks about the least willingly.

This is a truth that must be known and meditated upon if we

are to translate the usual commonplace of "moral forces" into precise concepts.

At the threshold of each of our military regulations, the importance of the moral forces is affirmed in a few eloquent sentences, but generally our cult does not go beyond this introductory invocation consecrated by tradition, and after the accomplishment of this rite, destined – it would seem – to render some distant divinity preparatory, one believes oneself entitled not to think about it anymore.

This is a serious mistake and to want, as is too often done, to study methods of instruction and combat procedures in a way that is somehow impersonal and independent of the "moral" combatant, is as unreasonable as building a machine without taking into account the driving force that must animate it.

We are taught that the psychic factors are preponderant in combat; this is not enough to say: strictly speaking, there are no others, because all the others, such as the perfection of the armament and the skill of the maneuver, act only indirectly, by the moral reactions which they provoke.

An important war occurring after a fairly long period of peace necessarily marks in military ideas a very clear reaction in favor of prudence. One has gone so far as to conclude from the accounts of the Transvaal war that, since no one can face the destructive power of modern machines, the direct offensive is henceforth only a costly utopia. If the events of the Far East have done justice to this exaggeration by showing that the frontal attack in front of the modern gun is not impossible, it is nevertheless proven that it has become extremely painful.

In these conditions, it seems that one should - since it is more difficult than in the past - find the combat more deadly; the statistics affirm the opposite. Should we conclude that the witnesses are wrong? Certainly not, and it would be a mistake to rely unreservedly on the "eloquence of the figures."

The immediate impression of the combatants is our only first-hand document and must be taken as true, but the interpretation they give is often inaccurate. So it is not the example of tactical procedures, often improvised under fire and which may not suit us very well, that we should ask of them, but the exact notion of what we can obtain from man in the face of today's danger.

The danger of death, always the same in combat, manifests itself in each era with a special physiognomy and the morale of combatants is affected even more by the form than by the materiality of the risk.

The figures which express this risk, in spite of their apparent rigor, have therefore for us less importance and reality than the observation of psychic facts and the saying of those who have seen. It is not the ell of the weapons used that controls the procedures and determines the conditions of the combat; it is the impression that these weapons make on the man.

The apparent contradiction between the assertions of the combatants who show us that combat is more difficult and more terrifying than ever and the statistical figures which prove it to be less deadly, brings us a striking confirmation of this.

The most remarkable and perhaps the most unexpected lesson of the recent battles will be that even today: "the human heart is the starting point in all things of war." It is in any case the one that seemed to us the most likely to throw some light on the difficult problem of infantry combat.

Chapter II – Principles of Offensive Combat

The recent experience of the Far East war allows us to stop discussing certain theories that came out of the British campaign in South Africa. The direct offensive is possible, we attack in front of the repeating rifle and smokeless powder. We will have no difficulty in recognizing that offensive infantry combat is difficult and costly and that it requires new procedures. Before studying these particularities, we must recall some principles that are beyond dispute after as well as before the last two wars.

The infantry has, we are told, two modes of action: "fire and forward movement." It would be more accurate to say that, in the offensive, the only mode of action of the infantry is: "the movement forward by fire," in order to highlight both the correlation and the relative importance of these two factors.

It is indeed important to state immediately that fire is only a means to enable forward movement. Forgetting this principle sometimes leads to the most deplorable aberrations. Experience shows that the often unreasonable and rarely absolutely conscious fear of being boarded is the real leaven of demoralization for the combatant, as soon as he loses the feeling of his superiority, and it would be a dangerous illusion to hope, by fire at a distance, to uproot solid troops from the position they are defending and from the trenches that cover them, if it were not for the fear of being boarded or turned.

Let us also note that forcing the enemy to give up the ground he occupies is the only sure sign of success and it is in this sense that we can say: To win is to advance.

It is therefore absolutely necessary, in order to obtain a decision, that the infantry advance on the enemy, and it can only advance by fire. In these conditions, the problem of the attack can be posed as follows: "how can the attacker establish himself at effective range with superior forces in front of the defense, take on it the superiority of fire, approach more and more so as to be able to finally reach the position with a leap"?

One point of this statement requires an immediate explanation. Since it is the necessary condition of success, what exactly is it to take the superiority of fire? Perhaps it would be prudent to be satisfied with a statement: "to have fire superiority is: in the offensive, to be able to advance, in spite of the enemy, at effective firing distances; in the defensive, to prevent the enemy from advancing."

However, let's try to be more precise.

From a certain distance, any troop seen – whatever its formation – is pinned down by the fire of the defender. But, if it manages by its own fire to extinguish or at least to hinder the fire of its adversary, to make him not fire anymore or to fire badly, it will be able to continue to advance. Its progression will be all the more easy and sure that it will hold the defender more completely under the depressing impression of an unequal fight. It will have the superiority of fire.

So, it is a fact: from a certain point on, the attacking infantry can no longer advance nor even show itself in a dispersed formation under the fire of a cold-blooded and comfortable opponent. In order to continue to advance, it must act on the enemy, subjecting him to fire that is effective enough to extinguish or at least make his fire uncertain.[*]

This critical moment of the combat where one can and must necessarily assert this first superiority depended until now, in great part, on the "practical scope" of the armament. With today's weapons, other factors come into play.

This distance was 100 meters at the beginning of the nineteenth century, 400 to 500 meters in 1870, it would have been 500 to 600 meters with the rifle model 1874. During the last wars, it was brought, we are told, towards 800-1000 meters.

It is likely that in a European war, whatever the improvements made to the rifle, the effective combat distance would not exceed this figure. For a long time, the value of the weaponry & almost had an influence on the width of this death zone. But, as we have seen, it is not at all at the extreme range of the weapon that corresponds the effective distance of combat. It is always close to the range below which a man pointing the barrel of his weapon at any point on the ground has a chance of firing a useful shot.

This is, roughly speaking, the blank target that a summary sighting over the barrel or, in our fusegates, over the aiming device in its usual position, gives; this blank target corresponding roughly to a completely dangerous trajectory or at least such that the deviation in height due to the weapon is negligible compared to the errors that come from the combatant.

Our current rifle, firing the 86 D cartridge, would give according to this rule at least 800 meters.

But then other factors intervene, which, as the zone widens, become more important and stop the indefinite extension of the "effective distance" of shooting. Among these factors, we can mention :

The training of men: with our present trajectories, the slightest error sends the bullet to such distances, that it is lost for the fight;

---

[*] It must be observed that very often, in front of a superior artillery, the infantry would not even reach the effective range of fire of the rifle – whereas, supported by an artillery more powerful or more skilful than that of the defense, it will be able in other circumstances to come much closer without firing. – Wanting to study here the combat of the infantry, we had, for the needs of the analysis, to consider the case where the two artilleries are about the same value.

The visual acuity and outdoor habits: if the Boers, hunters of the Veldt and herdsmen, could open an effective fire to 900-1,000 meters, it is quite probable that this range should be appreciably reduced with our men who do not have clearly at such a distance;

The ability to take advantage of the terrain: at 800-1,000 meters, the rapid movements of groups in diluted formation are very difficult to grasp and the slightest fold in the ground can serve as shelter.

It is rare in our countries to find firing ranges of 800-1,000 meters without shelter. One should avoid engaging in them.

In these conditions, one can, without implausibility, think that the critical point of the combat would occur "at the limit of the last covers below 800 meters."

Offensive infantry combat thus theoretically comprises two distinct periods:

During the first, with the help of diluted formations and a very careful use of the terrain, the attacker can progress in front of an opponent still possessing all his means;

During the second, no unit seen can advance without fighting, that is to say without having, by its fire, deprived the enemy of part of its means.

In practice, of course, these two phases are not so clearly defined. The approach march, at first easy, becomes more and more painful, difficult and dangerous as the moment approaches when the fire of the defense will become – if it is not extinguished at least in part – an insurmountable obstacle.

After having noted to what ordeal is subjected the man who engages in the field of the rifle, henceforth very widened, to laboriously make his way there and to buy each step at the risk of the life, we will perhaps have to admit that most often the human organism would be impotent to provide a similar effort.

It is in this sense that it could be said that normally, in open ground, a frontal attack of infantry under rifle fire is impossible.

The need to reduce this ordeal is therefore obvious. We know the means: to use as long as possible defilements by renouncing the direct attack of certain portions of the line, when the terrain does not lend itself to it;

To feed the fight with fresh troops and sometimes, in the interminable battles of today, to completely relieve the units engaged for too long;

To take advantage of the night to approach in order to start the fight at short distance, etc.

But these expedients themselves would be too often ineffective, if the infantry were reduced to its only means. In an important action, this isolation, moreover, will be quite exceptional and, to analyze too closely the combat procedures of the infantryman without taking into account the artillery, one risks making a mistake.

The artillery of the defense, in front of the first reserved zone (limited by the effective range of the rifle), will create a second one through which the march of the infantry will require great precautions.

Less regularly beaten, it is true, and seen from less close than that of the rifle, the domain of the cannon is much wider and the firing procedures of rapid-fire artillery can make it very dangerous.

The infantry of the attack, which will have to stay there and move for several hours sometimes, under the permanent threat of a burst, would have to undergo there – if it were left to its own strength – a very hard test and often sufficient to put it off. But another element intervenes: the artillery of the attack.

We will not discuss the use of the canon here. Let us only note once again that it is impossible to consider artillery combat independently of infantry combat.

There is only one combat, where each weapon plays its role in view of the common goal. To attack is to advance. The infantry must know that in order to advance it needs the help of its artillery; but the artillery must not ignore that its task in combat is summed up in this: to help by its fire the forward movement of its infantry. When it works for its own account and not with the immediate and direct aim of helping the infantry, its action is worthless. We find an interesting confirmation of this in the obvious uselessness of prolonged distant bombardments without immediate aim, so frequent in the English campaign and exaggerated again – it seems – in Manchuria.

Let us note that it is not enough to point out the uselessness of such demonstrations to make them disappear, and those who order them would probably recognize, in cold blood, that they are useless. – It is a perfectly logical moral phenomenon.

Two dogs before fighting try to scare each other by their barking. Homer's heroes used to bark at each other – out of range of the strokes – before they came to blows. Today, we insult each other with cannon fire, and preferably with cannons that reach farther than those on the other side.

Although these practices are not reasonable, they are nonetheless natural. One feels the need to reassure oneself by a demonstration of force with the hope of intimidating the adversary, of hurting him without risking anything, so as to avoid the ordeal of a real fight.

If, therefore, one wishes to restrict the use of ammunition and to renounce these useless demonstrations, which are counterproductive and, above all, show a lack of self-control, it will not be enough not to order them; one must prevent them by taking judicious precautions.

Chapter III – Approaches

The marching procedures imposed by circumstances on the British during the second period of the South African campaign, as well as the information already collected on the paths of the Japanese in the offensive, document the difficulty of the approaches in front of today's rifle. Two points summarize the question:

Continuous use and quite frequent failure of night operations;

Impossibility, in daytime approaches, of marching in an "ordered system," even if it is very open.

Let us examine briefly which consequences it is advisable to retain in view of the instruction.

I – Night operations

In the numerous night operations, so often followed by failure, that we are informed of – and in particular in the first period of the South African campaign, – it is easy to note serious errors of execution; but one is struck especially by this much more interesting fact that very often those who ordered them do not seem to have realized what one "can do at night."

Night operations must be the object of more careful study and more frequent exercises than in the past for two reasons:
1. Our entire combat technique is increasingly summarized in the use of fire to act on the enemy and in the use of terrain to avoid the effects of fire. At night, in the open country, fire only counts as a scarecrow; it follows that night combat, whose means have not changed, differs more and more from day combat;
2. The current rifle makes combat so difficult and repulsive for the infantry, that we use all the means that seem appropriate to avoid it. Attacking at night naturally seems to be the best way to restore the balance, since fire no longer counts. The experience of the English and especially the events of the Russo-Japanese war show how tyrannical this tendency becomes and how it leads to real abuses.

It is therefore extremely important for us – since like others we will necessarily use and be inclined to abuse night combat – to fix our ideas on the procedures to be used in night operations and even more so on what should be required of these operations.

The conditions of night combat forbid the engagement of an affair requiring the liaison of efforts and the intervention, during the action, of the higher command. The difficulties of leading the troops and their very unstable moral equilibrium require that the operation be prepared in advance and make it particularly dangerous to waver, hesitate or modify the program during the execution.

It follows that any night operation must have a precise, limited and very exactly defined goal. Its objective will almost always be: "to occupy a point of the ground and to keep it."

A night attack can and must be articulated in depth, that is to say, it must be carried out by several groups of troops having the same objective and following the same route. The leading group fights; the others replace it if it fails and, above all, occupy the conquered ground. There is therefore no combination, but a succession of efforts.

The objective to be reached is always determined (removal of a post, of a large guard, of an important point of the terrain). If the driver of a night attack is not exactly oriented in advance, he will himself, before setting off, determine the point he wants to reach, reserving the right to choose another one after having reached the first.

When aiming at several points at the same time, as it is impossible to mount a large action, for lack of being able to link the parts, it is necessary to have as many distinct attacks as different objectives, each of them going straight to its goal. There is nothing to prevent several efforts, that is to say, to direct several distinct attacks by different routes to the same point; but these attacks will not be "linked." The fixing of departure times is the only possible coordination.

If it is no longer a question of combat, but of the approach march of a unit of some importance, with the aim of gaining time, of crossing a zone beaten by fire, of occupying an advantageous cover close to the enemy, etc., it is necessary to have determined exactly in advance the point of the terrain that each column must reach and to have taken precautions to avoid any surprise during the movement; it is finally necessary to be certain not to find oneself, when the day comes, in a bad posture to fight.

The movement will therefore be preceded by reconnaissance that is as exact as possible; it will be carried out behind a solid stationary security service formed by detachments occupying in advance the points to be reached or installed in front.

Most often a night operation will include both combat and approach of large units. The first step will be to remove the enemy posts, the possession of which will allow to occupy in force certain zones of ground or important points in order to facilitate the following day's combat.

It can be seen that, in short, the night operation is a maneuver. It prepares the battle by allowing it to be engaged more closely or under better conditions, but, no more than any other maneuver, it cannot dispense with it. If sometimes the success of a night attack on a point of the battlefield is sufficient to decide the retreat of the enemy, it is because of the consequences that the occupation of this point could have for the daytime fight. Recognizing that he would be forced to fight in disadvantageous conditions, the adversary prefers to give up.

As far as the combat procedures are concerned, we shall remember the following:

At night one always acts "assembled"; it would be impossible to do otherwise.

The combat itself - although one can approach each other at bayonet range - is reduced to very little. All its value lies in the moral impression produced on the defender by the abruptness of the attack. It has little chance of success if it does not succeed at first.

The only method of combat, at night, is therefore not the shock, because there is no shock effect, but the immediate threat of boarding occurring in an unexpected and abrupt manner. One can say that without "surprise" there is no night attack.

A distinction must be made between field operations – the only ones we are dealing with here – and siege operations carried out under very different conditions. Adversaries stay for weeks at a very short distance, know every clod of earth in the space between them, and may frequently employ artificial means, such as spotted fire or searchlights. This remark is not useless in the study of the innumerable night operations carried out in Manchuria. The adversaries found themselves, on certain points and for long periods, in conditions similar to those of siege warfare, whose procedures they used.

Having made this reservation concerning the special operations of siege warfare, let us repeat that, in field warfare, night operations are intended to prepare for combat; they do not replace it.

II – Daytime Approaches

The British in South Africa, at the beginning of the war, ignored approaches. In spite of the total change in their methods during the course of the operations, we will have – even in the second period of the campaign – only negative lessons to ask of them.

Their preparatory marches for combat in thin successive lines deployed in advance on a disproportionate front can suit neither our impressionable men, nor our cut off countries, in front of an active adversary and equipped with rapid-fire artillery. Moreover, no advantage redeems the disadvantages of this dispersion, since at the first shots of the rifle there is nothing left of this system. The impressions produced on a witness by the aspect of the combat at the moment when the fire begins to be felt are interesting. – Let us summarize it, by observing that the accounts coming from Manchuria give the same note.

"The path is made by jumps, which are executed by more or less numerous groups, without regularity. The line broke up into sections that clumped together behind all the shelters; the open parts of the terrain were avoided."

"At first, the English officers, taking advantage of a lull, tried to lead their group, by their example, from one shelter to another; some men, always the same, were slow to follow them and the troop melted away. They got into the habit of sending an officer and a few volunteers to the next shelter in advance, reserving the right to watch the movement and to push the stragglers."

"On the combat line, they tried to use the ground as completely as possible. It is the shelters that regulate the march; squads, sections, whole companies come to huddle behind each of them; without order, without symmetry."

"The aspect of combat brings out the irresistible fascination for the man under fire, of the group and the shelter."

"This march from obstacle to obstacle lasts thus until a distance usually between 1,000 and 800 meters from the enemy, who is always invisible. – At this point, the fractions of the line in front of them on relatively uncovered terrain are immobilized."

"The clues that mark this moment of the battle are as follows: Any collective movement in the line of battle causes a redoubling of the enemy fusillade. –– The men lying down no longer tolerate a man standing near them and the officers must take the same position. It is impossible to collect the wounded without attracting a hail of bullets."

This is what a regular formation becomes at the first shots. We will therefore refrain from attaching any virtue to the form of a rigid system – even if it is, as the British know, crumbled to the point of exaggeration – and we will only mention the serious disadvantages of this crumbling.

Premature and excessive deployment weakens the attack. It is necessary to use the ground as long as one can to march "in troops" and to form one's line of combat only as late as possible.

The care to maintain cohesion is all the more imperative as the morale of the combatant is more unstable.

The opening of fire always delays the forward movement; a parsimonious and distant fire has no offensive value, it slows down the march without acting on the enemy. The approaches will therefore be pushed until it becomes impossible to advance without acting on the enemy.

The habit of marching from great distances in thin lines or fractions of lines under the pretext that this formation is less vulnerable is not to be encouraged. It is not conducive to cohesion, and it also facilitates the premature opening of fire. Moreover, when it comes to weak groups, their theoretical vulnerability does not matter. The main thing in the approaches – both in front of the gun and the rifle – is to make the enemy's fire difficult and unsafe by the complete exploitation of the terrain, the little visibility of the objectives presented and the irregularity of their appearances.

As far as we can judge, this is how the Japanese infantry understood it.

How, in these conditions, can we orient our training towards approaches?

Let us first observe that, for us, any march during which we seek to gain ground without fighting will be an approach march; whether it is a question of support in the rear of the line of combat or of elements in the front line before the opening of fire.

The combatant during the approaches, still capable of thoughtful attention, will obey to a fairly large extent the direction of his leaders and apply the procedures learned. The training of maneuvers can thus be done under conditions close enough to reality to give the men and the cadres correct ideas and habits that can be used at the moment of need; – it follows that the teaching of the procedures of the route will take an important place in the whole of our preparation.

As in all matters pertaining to combat, considerations of "morale" must take precedence. If, in approach marches, the precautions taken have the immediate aim of avoiding losses, it is because of the influence that these losses can exert on the morale of the troop; there are other [actors that should not be neglected and the marching procedures most likely to reduce the number of losses are not in all circumstances the best.

We frequently use, for example, and perhaps abuse a little the "filtered" movements man by man. Nothing better when – the terrain being suitable – one can hope to deceive the enemy's surveillance and that the soldier, not having yet been afraid, walks isolated without reluctance and effortlessly detaches himself from the ground and the group.

But as soon as the bullets whistle less rarely, it will be prudent – even for a running leap – to have several men leave at once. Our soldier does not like to fight alone; to show his comrades that he is not afraid is a need for him, and sometimes the whole group will be made to advance in one leap, whereas each man would be unable to make the same leap alone.

Even at great distances and on suitable terrain, very open formations should only be momentary. With troops like ours, whose cohesion is relatively unstable, it is important to break the bonds of the group as late as possible, and it would be a real danger for us to make men march and station for a long time in a row, dispersed at large intervals.

We must also take into account the enormous loss of time caused by exaggerated filtering. Time can become a decisive factor. The usual weakness of our numbers prevents us from giving it the importance it deserves.

All our approach formations will be summarized in a certain number of autonomous groups more or less strong according to the ground and the circumstances. Their movement will be coordinated not by intervals and distances to be kept strictly, but by a general direction known to all and by the indication of successive stopping points well marked on the ground, where the leader will be able to find and take back his troop. Each group, using the terrain for its own purposes, will march together as often as possible, breaking up into "human dust" only for the time strictly necessary to move from one shelter to another.

In practice, the companies will remain together as long as the terrain will allow them to walk to the shelter, only spreading out for the time necessary to cross a dangerous passage.

It is only when this grouped march becomes too dangerous or too slow that the unit will resolve itself into more manageable groups. (The half warfare section of twenty to twenty-five men seems to constitute a convenient group for approaches and combat).

Although studying here only the form and procedures of the direct infantry attack without addressing the overall tactics of the battlefield, a remark is necessary to avoid very easy misunderstandings.

The direct attack by force is not the whole battle. The period of the approaches, such as we have defined it, is precisely characterized by the fact that the use of the ground and the skill of the maneuver make it possible to advance without intercepting the enemy's resistance directly by fire. One must understand in this period the engagement of the vanguards, made so uncertain and so painful by the rapid fire without smoke.

This important question is beyond our scope. Let's just note that it is a question of sweeping away the enemy's security elements and thwarting his delaying tactics, in order to determine without delay his true line of resistance. It would therefore be playing into the opponent's hands to persist in removing each point of resistance encountered by a direct and concentrated fight that the power of fire always makes very laborious.

The game of the vanguard and the first troops engaged, in front of a resistance, will always be the automatic enlargement, the sliding towards the wings of the elements which follow the fraction hooked from the front. If the point of resistance is isolated, it falls before the investment very quickly obtained; if this point is part of a position with a narrow front, the wings are soon spotted; if it is finally a large and solid line, the necessary recognition of this line is hastened by the almost simultaneous engagement of several fractions on a large front.

A decided offensive is thus characterized, in the period of engagement, by the immediate enlargement aiming at the investment. But when one has, by this means, cleared the ground and finds oneself face to face with an enemy who does not allow himself to be maneuvered, one must come to a direct attack, and there, as we shall see, there is no power without successive efforts and without depth.

This affirmation of the necessity of the direct attack – in contradiction to the ideas of those who want to see the whole fight in the enveloping of the flanks, i.e., in the maneuver – in no way prejudges the form that, as a whole, the battle will take. Experience, in agreement with common sense, proves that, for the offensive, the enveloping form is by far the most frequent and the most advantageous.

Chapter IV – Combat at Effective Distance of Shooting

If the documents abound precise and concordant on the subject of the approaches, it is not any more of it even when it is about the "full combat."

From the moment when the deadly fight begins at a good shooting distance, the accounts become incomplete and the descriptions vague. One feels that the actors, absorbed by the tension of all their faculties towards the goal, by the violent and continuous impression of the danger, could only keep of this crisis an overall impression and badly coordinated memories.

At this moment, moreover, the man even cultivated does not obey any more that partially the reasoned councils of his intelligence: he acts under the direct impulse of some simple and strong feelings, some natural the others acquired by the education and the training. No rule, no formula, can henceforth guide him in this hard test.

Will we conclude that our work of preparation to the war stops at the threshold of this "zone of death" and that it is necessary for the last act to rely on the qualities of the soldier?

This is somewhat the impression that emerges from certain

military writings that have emerged from the South African war. This is a serious exaggeration. If it is imprudent and moreover useless to look for fixed rules and general formulas, it does not follow that it is impossible to develop and to direct in view of the combat, by a rational training, the faculties of the soldiers and the executives.

It is precisely the bases of this training that it is interesting for us to research.

From the facts themselves, as well as from the impressions noted by the witnesses, four principal observations emerge:

I. Impossibility of advancing on a seen ground, at effective distance of shooting, without having acted beforehand on the enemy by its fire;

II. Almost insurmountable difficulty to lead the combat, whose progress seems to depend solely on the initiative and vigor of the lower cadres and soldiers;

III. Adhesion to the ground and difficulty in moving the troops on the battlefield;

IV. Demoralizing effect of combat, nervous exhaustion of the combatants, resulting in: the rapid and complete wear and tear of the troops involved, the enormous increase in the duration of combat and the increasing importance of moral factors.

We will examine each of these observations, noting in passing the consequences that should be retained for our practical use, but reserving, to group them at the end and study them in a better light, those that concern the *execution of fire*.

I – Impossibility of advancing & effective firing distance without having acted upon the enemy by his fire

One of the most considerable facts of the campaign of the English in the south of Africa is the almost absolute incapacity of their troops to advance in front of the rifle, at effective firing distance. We know the cause: their fire was insufficient to make the adversary suffer seriously or to suppress his fire. By studying the few attacks that they succeeded in, we can see that these are the ones where, due to the circumstances, they were able to cause losses to the Boer fighters and prevent them from firing correctly.

It is nonetheless proven that fire superiority is usually very difficult to take in today's combat and that it is impossible to take head-on, by the methods of field warfare, a position defended by men who cannot be reached. The information that reaches us from the Far East only confirms this observation; but it also demonstrates, without the need for further discussion, that the defender is not always elusive and that the direct attack can succeed.

The frequent invisibility of the adversary at effective firing distance is certainly one of the most notable features of our modern combat. Not to be seen becomes a capital advantage, and what one reports of the customs of the artillery in the Far East towards the end of the war shows us how much the combatants feel it.

The defense will not fail to take advantage of it.

We touch there a critical point which the attack will exceed only at the price of great efforts and a considerable waste of time. Experience proves moreover that very often it will not succeed.

In order to gain fire superiority, that is to say, to demoralize the enemy, it is necessary to reach him by his fire. This requires three things:

Bringing one's troops in good shape to a practical firing distance;

To discover the enemy;

Firing effectively.

We have said, in dealing with approaches, by what procedures one can hope to overcome the considerable difficulties of making contact and establishing oneself at firing distance. But, whatever the skill of the routes, it is most often between 500 and 900 meters that we will have to start the fight; it is therefore at these distances that we will have to discover an enemy who is hiding and reach him by our fire.

It is necessary to insist all the more that the extreme difficulty to shoot effectively on the insufficient and distant objectives that a prudent enemy will present is not sufficiently known. Our maneuvering habits can only distort ideas on this subject, and this point is almost always sacrificed in our training, because it requires a lot of care and time, and the results are difficult to observe.

The necessity of a very serious training of the eye by frequent exercises of "research of objectives" and aims at the distances of combat (500-800 meters) must constitute for us one of the important lessons of the recent wars.

But it is not just a matter of taking fire superiority in a duel at a distance. Fire is only a means to ensure forward movement.

With the distances of combat that the effective range of our current weapons allows, the attack will require a lot of time and it is not only at the beginning, but during all its duration, that one must dominate the adversary; one will thus have to have always in line and firing a number of rifles appreciably superior to that of the adversary.

It is the shooting of the men stopped that makes possible the march of those who advance. The theoretical solution of the problem would be to have only a number of men marching at a time, calculated in such a way that the number of rifles firing from a firm position would remain sufficient to dominate the rifles of the defense.

The passage to the practice is embarrassing. One can, it is true, on the field of combat imagine combinations such that at each moment the proportion of men in motion is limited; and, from the point of view of training, these exercises are not useless to make the soldiers and the cadres understand that the possibility, for some of them, of progressing depends absolutely on the effectiveness of the fire of others. But it is important to give these simulacra only the value that they really have.

On the battlefield, such an expedient will no longer be appropriate; it will become quite impossible to regulate and direct the march of the echelons.

Each fraction of the line, each group, will be left to its own initiative and will have to distinguish, in a sort of instinctive way, the moment when an effort forward can and must be attempted.

Only men possessed by the desire to win, driven by the need to march on the obstacle and to reach the enemy, which constitutes the warrior spirit, trained to respect the order received and the solidarity of the battlefield, that is to say, animated by the military spirit, can succeed.

This double task (to maintain the superiority of fire and to continue to gain ground in front) would often exceed, it must be recognized, the forces of the infantry without the assistance of the artillery.

It is true that it can be alleviated in certain cases, by specializing the work at least temporarily. When the circumstances lend themselves to it, certain units installed in cover and at good range can be charged with taking the superiority of fire, without any other concern than that of holding the defender under heavy and carefully adjusted fire.

Other fractions, during this duel with the rifle, slipping into the depressions, taking advantage of the cover, will try to progress without attracting attention until the assault distance or at least until a suitable position to establish, closer to the enemy and in better conditions, a new line of fire.

This method, which to some extent allows the command to direct the combat, can unfortunately only be applied with success under special conditions, in particular in very uneven terrain, where it becomes the rule.

Most often, therefore, the infantry in serious combat, in normal terrain, would be powerless to maintain its fire superiority while gaining ground in front.

It is to the collaboration of the artillery that one must appeal. Thanks to its range, the curvature of its trajectories and the safety of its adjustment, it will always be able to fire over the moving troops or establish itself on the flanks. Its action is not limited to certain phases of the battle, it is present at all times. It is the particular role of the cannon to constitute in the attack this fixed element of fire superiority, necessary to maintain control over the enemy during all the time that lasts the laborious exodus of the infantryman.

A special artillery will therefore be designated for each infantry attack. From that moment on, it precedes with its fire each step of "its infantry" and its main objective is always the enemy troop, cannon or rifle, which at the moment in question is firing on this infantry.

Whatever the means used to obtain and maintain fire superiority while gaining ground, the infantry wears out in this task, its fighting capacity dulls, its living strength diminishes very quickly (losses, fatigue, moral depression...).

To want to carry out a serious attack until the end with the same men without reinforcing its line of combat – however strongly constituted it may be at the beginning – is a utopia. This line must be supplied materially and morally by fresh troops.

This supply is very difficult, or cannot be denied, and bringing reserves to the line of fire at the right time is a scabrous problem.

The possibility of these reinforcements making their way to safety and reaching the front without too many casualties has even seemed so doubtful that some critics of the South African war have proposed solving the problem by simply super-sizing the reinforcements. On the pretext that there had never been a "push" from the rear into the line of fire, they proclaimed the futility of reserving troops and attacking in depth.

Their reasoning is based on an equivocation, and one could, even in the Transvaal War, cite many cases where the arrival of fresh troops made it possible to continue and succeed in an attack, which had sometimes been stopped for several hours.

This often effective intervention does not usually result, it is true, in a sudden thrust, and one may believe that almost never will the line of battle be pushed or driven forward by reserves from the rear – it will only be supplied with men, reinforced in the true sense of the word.

The thrusting or driving forward by the material momentum of fresh troops is hardly to be expected except in certain rare circumstances.

It is necessary, indeed, for this push to occur:

That the reinforcing troops reach the chain in coherent and relatively tight formations and that the terrain and the circumstances of the battle lend themselves to an overall movement, at least on the portion of the line where the reinforcement is made.

These circumstances will hardly present themselves except in a sudden attack launched from close quarters with a considerable superiority and immediately following a preparation by fire, short perhaps, but very energetic.

The same effect can be produced at the moment of the assault in front of an adversary close enough to demoralization that the appearance of a troop in order is sufficient to definitively break the balance.

All the shallow attacks we find in recent wars have failed – the observation has its value. But perhaps it is simply that they were not strong enough to begin with, and the best thing to do then would be to immediately put enough people on the line to fight to the end.

This solution is not acceptable. The terrain, in a serious attack, would not be sufficient for deployment. Lines that are too dense and that can only move with difficulty and only imperfectly, would suffer heavy losses without their fire becoming more effective, because the men, being mutually embarrassed and poorly sheltered, would fire less quickly and more poorly.

On an attack front, one will usually find only a limited number of advantageous routes. These paths will be successively exploited by the front line groups, then by the reinforcements. If the first line is formed too strongly at the outset for all the elements to profit, those of them who will be obliged to use the uncovered parts of the ground, soon immobilized at a long distance, will find themselves spent without profit.

One can consider these sheltered marching areas as channels to feed the battlefield. When it will be necessary to deploy to fight, the line of combat will be formed by blooming at the outlet of each of the paths followed; then the troops continuing to refine by the same ways, the line of fire will become, in the vicinity of these paths, strong enough to take the necessary superiority and gain ground. It will form there like the points of wear or, if one wants, the teeth of the attack.

It can be seen that the conception of infantry combat using the terrain is incompatible with the formation at long distance of a single and very dense line.

On the other hand, by immediately putting everyone in line, one would not obtain that indispensable moral comfort produced by the arrival of troops tons until then relatively safe in the hands of their leaders, and not yet exhausted by the nervous exhaustion so characteristic of the current combat. Let us note finally another mission of the troops available at short distance. During a long and laborious attack, such as we can conceive it, it will be necessary at each step forward to consolidate the progress accomplished, by occupying without delay the conquered support points.

This task falls to the tired and disordered troops who have just made a violent effort. But it is then necessary that other troops are ready to overtake them as quickly as possible to take over the fight.

Maintaining the power of fire while gaining ground in front of the enemy is the main problem of offensive combat. This problem can only be solved by the union of arms and by an effort of increasing energy produced by the reinforcement, during the fight, of the forces of the attack.

It remains to be examined in what form this action by fire will be presented as a whole.

We have tried to find in the rare manifestations of the Boer offensive – remarkable manifestations, moreover – the revelation of a new combat and the type towards which our efforts must tend. This combat is characterized on the attacking side by a permanent superiority, obtained thanks to a continuous and uninterrupted fire, allowing the attackers to gain ground step by step, individually and, as it were, by capillary action, each one alternating for his own account a few rifle shots with a leap of a few meters, from one shelter to another.

This is obviously a very interesting combat procedure. Rarely used before the South African war (although a few examples can be found), it represents the usual way of the Boers in the offensive and has often succeeded them.

Experience proves therefore that it is practical in certain cases for men with a temperament similar to that of the Burghers.

Will it normally be possible and advantageous for us in a great war? Tent the question is there.

The fact that it has not become generalized in the Far East and has not been – as far as we can tell – employed by the Japanese in circumstances analogous to those of our probable struggles dispenses us from a detailed discussion.

Let us only note that this individualistic procedure would not be well suited to our young soldiers. They will have an imperative need to group together, to be encouraged to feel that they are not fighting alone.

Moreover, our lines will be much denser; the combatants and even the very weak groups will not be able to detach themselves from them to go forward while their immediate neighbors are firing.

What will be the physiognomy of our combat?

We must discard the individual leap as the usual mode of progression. On our battle lines, the "group" will replace the man and it is to the group leader that the initiative and the direction of the movement will belong.

Initially formed as regular units (sections or half-sections), the combat groups will sometimes lose all regularity in the course of combat. Their strength will vary and their value will depend largely on the man, rank or not, who will momentarily be followed and obeyed.

The line being thus formed of groups, will these groups act each one on its own account without any other link than the common objective giving to the whole movement and fire a continuous appearance? This process – continuation of the usual method of approaches – has its value when the groups are widely spaced in such a way that those who walk do not come at every moment to mask the fire of their neighbors. This part of the fight escapes any rule and any direction. Those who can, either because they have a stronger morale or because the terrain favors them, will advance.

But very often the combat groups will be too tight for each of them to "take off" without hindering the firing of the others, and the fractions of the line that have stopped firing to advance, as well as the elements that have stopped to fire, will then have to be quite wide. The fragmentation of the front into sections that can move with relative independence and without forcing the neighboring elements to remain silent will almost always be determined by the compartmentalization of the terrain or by some accidental gap in the line.

From the fact that, in order to make forward movement possible, the fire will have to be extinguished on a notable fraction of the front, it should not be concluded that this fraction will move forward in one go. Very often, on the contrary, it will move from one position to another in small groups, making the best use of the terrain, several of them sometimes following each other in the same path and each of them having no other concern than to reform the line in front. During this movement, which was sometimes quite long, it seemed that at this point they were attacking without firing, and this is precisely the impression reported by certain witnesses of some Japanese attacks.

It is in these crises that the rapid fire artillery will be able to help its infantry and to supplement by the acceleration of its fire the momentarily extinguished or attenuated infantry fire.

After this sustained effort until exhaustion of living force, our attack will come to cling to some accident of the ground. Its impotence to push further will produce a momentary lull during which the artillery will be silent and the relatively sheltered infantry will spare its fire as much as possible.

It is then that the leader, towards the points where he intends to push his advantage, will route new troops following the same defile routes as the first. Their arrival within range of the battle line will usually be the signal for the artillery to resume firing in bursts. The chain thus warned will sharpen its fire and the reinforcements will take advantage of this to move to the line, in order to determine a resumption of the forward progression.

Even in the absence of available reserves, after a period of calm and forced halt during which the troops will have been able to breathe and recover, the driver of an attack will often attempt to make a new effort. The action of vigorous officers, having the confidence of the soldier, will have to partly replace, on the chain, the absent reinforcements.

But how to give the impulse?

The personal action of the leader on the line of combat would necessarily be limited to a few men, the orders that he will send will reach only in an uncertain way. There is a serious difficulty here.

It is perhaps the rapid-fire artillery that will often solve it. By making it, after a period of silence, resume a vigorous fire, one will give the combatants, at the same time as the signal to make a new effort, the material help and the moral comfort which they will need.

Is this methodical process of progression that we have just studied, with its slow action and the strict economy of its means, the whole fight and will it always suffice to provoke a decision?

It will sometimes be enough. But in front of an enemy well endowed with courage and means, something else is needed.

After long hours, this "wear and tear" combat will bring the adversaries front to front at a distance more or less great according to the terrain and the circumstances, but such that from now on – if a maneuver does not decide the premature retreat of the defender – any partial effort to slowly gain ground by small fractions will become dangerous enough to be practically impossible. The fire and mutual wear and tear will then sometimes continue for a very long time without serious result, because the attack will no longer advance and the forward movement alone is decisive.

To get past this, it is necessary to advance; this can only be done brutally, without concern for losses, without economy. It is the attack of a strong force. The Russo-Japanese war, by showing that the frontal attack, with brute force, is necessary and possible, exempts us from any discussion. But one can ask oneself why – supported by the experience we have declared inadmissible in the course of the fight what we affirm possible and necessary at the moment when the danger is the greatest.

These rapid forward movements of a large number of men at a time, without concern for losses, are necessary at this moment because there is no other way to advance and it is necessary to advance. They are only possible, moreover, if the elfort to be provided, which can quickly become decisive, is of short duration. This requires:

That the already shaken enemy presents only a weak resistance to demoralization;

That the attack has a very marked moral and material superiority;

Finally, that the distance is relatively short. The principle, moreover, does not change and it is always fire that ensures the movement.

In these special circumstances, one can foresee – immediately following a preparation by fire as violent as possible and while the fire, at least that of the artillery, continues as far as possible – jumps of a whole dense line or broad echelons.

This line will be formed of groups or swarms, each one trained freely by its leader and alternating jumps at a run with short stops to catch their breath, until the moment when, some accident of the ground presenting itself, what remains will come to cling to it. A second line, following at short distance and formed like the first one of small packets using the ground, will come to join it, to reinforce it and to carry along its debris in front... and so on within the limit of the means available.

In this crisis, one can hardly count on the fire of the attacking groups; even if they could fire during the stops, their fire would have little value. The less they fire, the faster the movement will be, and this is the main element of success, for such an effort cannot be prolonged.

Any infantry attack carried out to the full has as its necessary end this total effort characterized by the concentration, on a chosen objective, of all available means and their violent use, without economy or ulterior motive. This brutal thrust, of increasing intensity, leads to the assault which quickly leads to a break in the balance in one direction or the other, a decision. Each of the numerous partial fights of which a battle is composed thus comprises a final crisis which one could say decisive.

Usually, when we talk about the "decisive attack," we mean the attack wanted and prepared by the leader with the intention of deciding the outcome of the battle.

The discussion of this question is a matter of general battlefield tactics and is beyond our scope. Let us only note that it cannot come to the mind of any reasonable man to make of it a special fight with particular form.

The decisive attack is characterized only by the desired concentration of the means at one's disposal in front of a chosen objective, occupied by an enemy already worn out, with the intention of obtaining at all costs a decision which one hopes will be definitive.

The "mass" of the decisive attack is thus in sum only a

reservoir of forces established at a short distance from the enemy and when one speaks of "shock," it is a moral shock.

II – Extreme difficulty to direct the fight and to give orders

One of the impressions most regularly recorded by witnesses of recent battles is the almost complete impossibility of conducting combat on the fire league. The junior officers obliged to hide like their men can only exercise their action in a small radius.

One observes moreover that the preliminaries, the approaches are described in a clear and precise way in their accounts, but that from the moment when one really fights at effective distance, the details become less precise and the indications more vague. The impression that emerges is that everyone does what they can; no more order, no more regularity, no more method. The value of the fight becomes the main actor of the success.

This impression is not new and it has always been so. In its acute crisis, the fight escapes from any rule, from any direction to obey only some general laws.

In the soul of the combatant, intoxicated by the training of the example, dizzy from the tumult, excited by the danger, exhausted by the fatigue, the morale sometimes exalted to the point of heroism or depressed to the point of abruptness, there is only one feeling that is powerful enough to be translated into acts: the instinct of conservation. Depending on the circumstances, the instinct of self-preservation manifests itself in this crisis sometimes by anger and the irrational desire to join the enemy to destroy him, sometimes by fear.

Each one executes then almost mechanically and all the more skillfully as the training has marked him more deeply, the movements ordered by the one of the two feelings which dominates: to draw, to run, to hide... As long as the resultant is positive – that is to say, as long as the tome pushing the fighter towards the enemy remains the strongest – one advances.

We knew all this. Does this mean that in this respect the last wars have taught us nothing?

On the contrary, they bring us an important contribution. The effectiveness of the rifle is practically increased and it results that the critical phase of the combat during which each combatant will have to draw in himself the necessary living force to advance, lasts longer.

This is not a negligible point. In the past, up to 200 paces from the enemy, the soldiers in close ranks, elbow to elbow, marched as a coherent troop and obeyed the commands of their officers, who only disbanded them at the last moment. The violent crisis of individual effort lasted only a few minutes.

In 1870, this dissolution of direct command could be delayed most often until 400-500 meters from the enemy.

Now it will be necessary to abandon sometimes to 800-900 meters of the enemy the engagement of combat, to the chance of the circumstances and to the value of the man.

During this long period the direct action of the officers on the line of fire becoming very narrow they will act only as trainers, as example givers. It is therefore rather their moral vigor and their character than their intellectual superiority that will enable junior officers to group their men around them, to dominate them and to sustain them in this ordeal.

Two conclusions arise.

1. When one speaks of "direction of the combat":

For the command, it is not a question of leading the men who are fighting at an effective distance of fire, but only of engaging them methodically in a good direction, as and when necessary, taking into account their offensive capacity and the result to be obtained.

For the junior officer, it is above all a question of setting an example, inspiring confidence and suggesting to the soldiers the execution of certain practices that the training will have made them familiar with.

There is no other "direction" of the fight.

2. It is impossible and useless to try to regulate in a formal way the procedures of combat or of marching under fire. The greatest initiative must be left to the executors. Each case requires a particular solution and such a method, impossible in certain circumstances of ground or "morale," will become excellent in another case.

Was it necessary to "improvise" on the battlefield?

Never, at the cost, the methodical instruction of the cadres and the training of the troops in view of the combat have been more necessary.

As a whole, as we have seen, combat is governed by a few very simple but very general principles, some of a psychological nature, others purely empirical.

This wide-meshed weave is our only guide in the work of preparing for combat; it is therefore essential to carefully examine its threads and to test its solidity.

Once this work is completed, is our task fulfilled and will it be sufficient to expose these few guiding principles, to entrust them to the meditations of all, and to leave it to each one to apply them?

Certainly not. – In the theoretical study of combat, the obligatory prudence of the conclusions and their imprecision easily leads to a kind of skepticism favoring laziness; the abuse of negative teachings – the only ones, in short, that can be given with certainty – the anemic spirit of decision. Moreover, a principle is a guide for the intelligence but is not a motor for the will; it must, to become direct source of act, be translated into rules.

The executor, soldier or rank, even if he possesses the experience and the open-mindedness necessary to make this translation correctly and to apply the principles to each particular case, will have neither the time nor the composure to improvise this solution. It would be impossible to obtain by this method the innate and quasi reflex reaction which must discipline one's acts and coordinate one's movements in the absence of a thoughtful decision.

This habit of responding to the suggestion of an idea or an impression by an immediate decision of the will or by an impulsive act of the body constitutes training.

Training can only be produced by a repetition of the same acts frequently enough so that the association between the command or suggestion and the movement or decision which must be its consequence, becomes tired in the unconscious without the intervention of reflection.

It is therefore not enough to state the few abstract principles, too often negative, which constitute the solid residue of a theoretical analysis of combat. To prepare men for combat, it is essential to teach them a positive doctrine and practical rules whose repeated application leads to training.

But how to establish these rules when – we have noted that combat escapes all regulation?

The difficulty is serious.

We have lived for a long time with an exaggerated regulation, very complicated to be practical and destructive to the rank of any initiative. In order to react against this excess, some people now pretend to stick to vague advice and believe that they can find a remedy for overly precise regulations in the suppression of all rules. Their error is no less dangerous.

It would be absurd to say to a man learning fencing, "When you make an assault you will begin with such and such an ump, you will continue with such and such a parry... and with that you are sure of success." But it would be no less so to tell him, under the pretext of sparing his initiative: "When you make an assault everything depends on the circumstances and the opponent. Here are the few principles on which the science of fencing rests; the rest is up to you."

A reasonable master will speak as follows to his pupil: "We will first make your limbs supple and familiar with the handling of your tool by simple and repeated exercises.

"Then you will be taught a number of moves: attacks, ripostes, parries. There may be others and nothing prevents you from seeking them out, but these are good ones, they are the fruit of long experience. When you have them completely in your hand, you can use them as you wish. It is a matter of temperament and circumstance.

"To enlighten your judgement and give you ideas, watch the masters, study foreign methods, take care of the technique of your art and the principles that dominate it."

Let us imitate this wise teacher.

The three stages of his teaching represent for us:

The individual training;

The collective training of the troop and the cadres;

The instruction of the officers.

There is nothing to say here about the training of the honest, whose necessity no one disputes, nor about the instruction of officers, which will never be too complete, too broad and too well reasoned, provided that positive instruction prevails over negative principles.

Remain the collective training. The subject, the limits and the form of this training are delicate to specify. It is the task of the drafters of regulations. We only want to affirm here that this training must exist and be based on rules.

Deployments, routing procedures, use of lights, safety measures, etc., can and must theoretically vary infinitely to correspond exactly to the circumstances of the moment.

In practice, it will be necessary to choose, after careful study, a certain number of procedures based on experience and in accordance with the aptitudes of our troops; these selected procedures will be transformed into rules which, through training, will become habits. Our cadres and our men will thus have at their disposal a certain number of "moves," of attack and defense procedures. The regulations will not, of course, affect the use of these procedures and the officer, the rank, whatever his level, when he will have neither the time nor the composure to work to measure, will choose the one which seems to him to be appropriate without having to worry about the execution. "If his method is not the best and is not worth in theory such other one that one could have imagined from scratch, in practice it will be more effective because it will be better executed and because one will have confidence in its value.

In this matter, everything is a matter of measure and a supporter of the "normal combat training," if it still exists, would find his account in what precedes.

Let us leave the publishers of normal training to their studies and note that the difference between what should be a matter of training and what, on the contrary, should only appear in the form of instruction or advice, is difficult but possible:

Training must exist - that is beyond doubt; what are the limits of its domain? - It can only reach those movements whose execution does not involve any reasoning.

For units with a staggered command (company, battalion), our regulations have wisely reduced training to a few elementary formations so that the leader can arrange his troop by a single command or warning without long explanations. – No more is needed.

The training of the homogeneous group obeying without intermediary to the same leader (which we still call Section School, although the section of 50 men is too strong by half to be manageable in combat) is the main part of the military training of our soldiers.

The group of 20 to 25 men must become the usual unit for marching, exercising and fighting. By a very thorough training but only on very simple things, we manage to give this group a cohesion, a flexibility, a personality which will make it the base of our infantry tactics.

The group will be the fighter of the future, provided that the rudimentary evolutions necessary to walk, hide, and fight become as familiar to each man as his individual movements.

Thanks to the very small number and the frequent repetition of these movements, the slightest suggestion will suffice to provoke them, whatever the men momentarily composing the group.

III – Ground Adhesion. Attraction of the group and the shelter

The adherence to the ground, the difficulty of moving the man in front of the rifle is a phenomenon that cannot be ignored by anyone who has led soldiers under fire, even if this fire is not very nourished and badly adjusted, as in most of our colonial battles.

The same is true for the attraction of the shelter, however inadequate and somewhat "theoretical" it is assumed to be. A small ditch, a hedge, a simple furrow attracts the combatant; he holds on better than in the open field and leaves it with difficulty.

The attraction of the group is also easy to observe. Left to themselves, the men join, curl up, seek the contact of the comrades and dread. above all the isolation.

Note that this last observation involves soldiers. The need to feel each other's elbows, to fight together is, in large part, the result of their collective training, of the military habits they have been made to take.

In reporting certain offensive actions conducted by the Boers, in which each man fought for himself without taking care of his neighbors, we have observed that this completely individualized combat can only be suitable for men gifted with warlike qualities of the first black and almost devoid of military training.

To go down this road and loosen the bonds of cohesion and common training, in order to respect the individuality of our men, would be a dangerous mistake. In spite of their remarkable personal qualities, the lack of cohesion and military spirit is one of the main causes of the Burghers' definitive failure. – It must not be forgotten.

The ineradicable tendency to stick to the ground will make it still more difficult and more repulsive for the troops to advance under the present rifle fire.

As we approach the enemy and his fire becomes more formidable, at the same time as the offensive capacity of the assailant diminishes as a result of his physical and moral exhaustion, it will become more difficult to get the men up and out of the shelter to which they are attached. It is therefore in the best interest to attempt this as little as possible and to make as many jumps as circumstances will allow.

Other reasons, it is true, seem in certain cases to advise very short jumps. We learn that it takes about ten seconds to make a burst arrive at its destination, when the adjustment is made. Consequently, in front of an artillery ready to shoot, each jump should not exceed 30 meters. Nothing should be exaggerated. In practice, it is the terrain that usually imposes the route to be taken and the fatigue of the men will limit the length of the route enough to make it useless to look for any other moderator.

At the training we will therefore make fairly short jumps, since they will most often be short in reality. But we will know that it would be better if they were long.

It would therefore be unreasonable to limit by fixed rules the initiative of the combatants; but it would be no less unreasonable, as we have shown, to leave it completely to the inspiration of the moment.

It is therefore our duty to choose in advance some practical procedures and, through training, to transform them into habits.

The procedures employed to gain ground forward must be appropriate to the temperament of the soldier and vary with his moral state; certain formations acceptable at the beginning of an action with troops whose morale is intact may no longer be possible at the height of the battle.

The attraction of the group is particularly powerful on our men. The French soldier has initiative, he is intelligent, independent in character but very sociable, impressionable to a fault and extremely accessible to suggestions of example. In short, he is well equipped for modern combat, provided that his needs are taken into account.

The leader's command, the immediate action of discipline has little hold on him (much less than on the German or Russian soldier, for example); he can therefore do without it without much trouble. But he has an absolute need not to feel alone, to fight "in society," and self-esteem is for him the driving force par excellence.

It follows that the French officer in combat must be an example setter rather than an order giver, and that our men will endure well the journeys in loose formation provided that they are always moved in small groups (4 or 5 men) instead of being sent in isolation, and that we take advantage of all the shelters to assemble them, even if it is only for a few minutes – the time to exchange a joke in order to show the others that we do not have to.

From these observations derive the important consequences already indicated in connection with the steps of approach; it is not useless to remember them:

The filtering man by man on the very openwork formations in which the soldier marches in isolation are possible for us only during the approaches; it will probably be necessary to give it up as soon as the fire is felt. The movements by small successive packs, dislocating the group to reform it further forward, will themselves become difficult under a violent fire and, in the last acts of the attack, all concern for prudence in the form of the jump necessarily disappears. The "follow me," the removal of the whole group in a single rush will then be the best and probably the only possible method of advancing.

Whatever the value of the men engaged, very few of them would be able to face such an ordeal in isolation: it is in collective action only that they will find the strength. The explanation of an assault as well as the secret of the panic is a matter of crowd psychology.

Moreover, there is no need to elaborate on "assault formations" and to refine on the technique of the actual attack.. All our efforts must be concentrated on the methods ready to lead, first by skillful routes and then by a methodical progression combined with fire, to a short distance from the enemy, troops still capable of fighting. – It is then only a matter of morale where the detail of the formations does not matter much more than the science of bayonet fencing. The manifest will to attack thoroughly, the conviction of the gesture decide the result. But it is still necessary that the enemy be impressed and that we show ourselves, since in the end it is a question of frightening him.

In our exercises, the figuration of the final attacks and assaults seems almost always unbelievable and somewhat ridiculous.

Perhaps the exact reproduction of some real and successful assaults would give us, in cold blood, an even more striking impression of implausibility and absurdity, since the only factors which are important are precisely those which we cannot take into account.

Also, while seeking to avoid too striking implausibilities and without being under any illusions on the technical value of the formations, it is good to often figure, in our maneuvers, assaults.

The man must keep this impression that any attack tends towards the assault and that the assault is possible.

IV – Demarcating effect of modern combat. Rapid wear and tear of the troops. Increasing importance of moral factors

The nervous exhaustion of the combatants and the demoralizing effect of the new combat are affirmed by all the witnesses of the last wars.

Their statement is corroborated by the facts. It is sufficient to cite the usual absence of pursuit – due to the impossibility of asking for a new effort from the troops – as well as the frequent examples of total and, as it were, lightning demoralization noted in units surprised by fire.

The rapidity and enormity of the losses cannot justify this extraordinary nervous exhaustion (the losses have most often remained lower than the average observed in the previous great battles.

The usual invisibility of the enemy and the feeling of the innateness of a randomly directed fire can be a first and very notable cause of nervousness.

It is enough to have witnessed a skirmish in the woods or to have been surprised by the smallest ambush in open, cut and difficult country to have experienced this irritation and to have felt the anguish produced by the feeling of being unable to reach the enemy, to hit him back blow for blow.

To this first cause is added in the modern combat the duration and the continuity of the danger.

The history of our great battles shows us the same men fighting the whole day and, when evening comes, in spite of enormous losses, still finding in themselves enough energy and strength to lead vigorous attacks or to pursue. The effort required by the acute crisis of the combat during which the soldier must spend without counting his physical and moral forces, was not less however than in our current fights. – But it was intermittent.

At the beginning of the nineteenth century, 200 or 300 meters of ceded ground were enough for a troop to find itself relatively safe, to recover and to fall back into the hands of its leaders. Rarely did this troop stay in the death zone for a long time. A battle represented then a succession of very violent but short efforts separated by relative rests. These efforts could therefore be renewed several times before fatigue and moral depression got the better of the combatants' energy.

It is no longer the same: the troops engaged at effective firing range must now, for each leap forward, for each inch of ground gained and sometimes for several hours, give this total effort which consists in sacrificing one's life. Soon the stops themselves do not constitute a rest and do not produce any nervous relaxation.

Men huddled in awkward positions behind inadequate

obstacles must... unceasingly listen to the deadly gust singing in their ears with the demoralizing sensation that the slightest movement constitutes a danger of death. – The human organism is not tempered to bear the danger with this intensity and especially with this continuity.

The fire of the defender does not destroy the assailant, but it demoralizes him in a way profound enough to suppress in him all capacity for effort.

This impression, let us note, is due more especially to the rifle fire. The sudden and short storms of artillery will perhaps be more capable of producing an immediate but momentary demoralization. The rifle alone brings about this special and lasting physiological result of nervous exhaustion, of stupefaction due to continuity.

Under artillery fire, a troop can be dispersed and very quickly neutralized; but, gathered under cover, it will often recover quite quickly. Only the troops having undergone rifle fire will be "worn out" sometimes for several days.

We have said and tried to demonstrate that if this difficulty is serious, it is not insoluble. There is, in truth, only one way to solve it, and that is to take the lead: demoralize the enemy and break his morale to prevent him from using his fire judiciously.

In any event, two lessons emerge from this fourth finding:

Faster and more complete wear and tear of the infantry in combat than in the past;

Increasing importance of moral factors.

This fact that the infantry wears out faster and more completely in combat only corroborates certain principles more than once already recorded:

Infantry combat requires strict economy, a methodical use of forces. A troop sent to fire is "spent," it should not be counted on for the day at least. It will give in the chosen direction the effort it is capable of, nothing more. If the result is not achieved, it will be necessary to spend another one.

In spite of some carefully exploited examples from which one wants to draw consequences which are not contained there, we will thus affirm that there cannot be a vigorous attack without supply coming from the rear. It follows that an attack system in order to allow this feeding will have to be deep.

But it is not only a question of bringing a certain number of men into the line of fire during the battle; they must be made to arrive there in fighting condition and less affected morally than the men they must support.

With the range and demoralizing effects of today's weapons, the conduct of front-line support becomes extremely difficult. If, in spite of careful use of the terrain, it becomes impossible to shelter them, if they suffer enough from the fire that their morale deteriorates significantly, the supports wear out without profit and no longer fulfill their purpose. We must make them fight.

There will therefore be supports behind the parts of the line where the terrain will allow them to be hidden; elsewhere, not. It is the terrain that will determine the points where the attack will be able to progress because it will be supported and fed there. We already knew that.

As for the reserved troops, the choice of their waiting places, the determination of the points where they can intervene, the moment of this intervention and especially the dosage of the forces to be spent in view of the goal to be reached, form without question the main task of the command in combat. This task is made more complicated by the requirements of the terrain which takes in our current engagements an importance that one should not try to attenuate. And there is really a "new fact" in this subordination more and more narrow of the tactical development of a combat to the forms and the covers of the ground.

It is still the last reserve which will be right and it is the assertion of an incontestable superiority on a point at least of the battlefield which will cause the rupture of moral balance necessary to make a winner and a loser. The economy of forces, that is to say, their use exactly proportionate to the goal, thus remains the supreme art of the leader. But his task becomes more complicated because his independence diminishes and in all his conceptions an indispensable collaborator intervenes: the field.

The reserves must be kept under cover and out of the fight, then brought to work still possessing all their offensive value. A skilful and prudent exploitation of the accidents of the ground will alone make it possible to obtain this result in front of the modern gun and rifle. And it will be the special role of the senior officers – since their direct action on the line of combat is now reduced to very little – to bring their troops there at least and to engage them in good conditions (to ensure their safety on station, to keep them safe from fire, to study and prepare the routes towards the enemy, and to lead the approach marches).

An officer who allows, by his incapacity or his lack of foresight, a troop which he is in charge of and on which the commander relies, to lose its strength along with its morale, is guilty of a fault which is always serious and often irreparable.

There remains the question of moral factors. Today, more than ever, it dominates all others.

The sophisticated implements of destruction are to be feared and taken into account not because they kill more – the opposite is true – but because they impress more. To use them will require more courage and firmness than ever before, and more than ever before victory or defeat will come down to a difference in morale.

Unfortunately, at a time when war demands from each man a higher morale and a firmer heart, the quality of the soldier in our European armies tends rather to decrease.

It is therefore not enough to affirm a theoretical faith in the superiority of moral forces; the duty of every officer is to seek and apply the practical consequences of his conviction. We leave aside here the study of the means to be employed, in the presence of the disturbing evolution of characters, to create and develop moral forces in time of peace; a similar investigation necessarily goes beyond the limits of this work.

But the preponderant importance, in the course of the combat, of the variations in the morale of the men, entails consequences in some technical way that it is important to retain. It is by making the examination of each military problem take into account the moral and physical conditions of the man in combat that we will have the chance to avoid building on the sand of theoretical speculations.

V – Fire – Shooting instruction

The study of offensive combat is the only reasonable basis that we can give to the instruction of shooting. So far we have tried, by observing the man in this combat, to determine why he must shoot and in what physical and moral conditions he will find himself to shoot.

The time has come to ask how he should shoot.

§1 - Combat Shooting

Until recently, the theory of collective shooting served as a basis for our combat shooting instruction. Let us briefly recall what it consists of.

It has been observed that on the polygon, the shooting of a moderately trained troop obeys, as a whole, certain mathematical laws – laws of collective shooting. It follows that in the indicated conditions (average training), the way of shooting of each man has no influence on the result of the shooting. This result depends only on the exact knowledge and the judicious exploitation of the laws of the collective shooting: single grouping distributed according to the laws of the dispersion with average point at distance of rise.

It is naturally the leader who will be in charge of interpreting and applying these laws in each particular case. The ability to "regulate," to "point" the fire of his troop will thus constitute the principal factor of effectiveness of the fire.

Let us admit, of course, the sincerity of the innumerable experiments made over the last twenty years and let us recognize that, at least in my case, things happen this way on the firing range. What conclusions are to be drawn from this? As there is, it is said, no reason why there should not be a relationship between the results of the range and those of the battlefield, one must admit that in combat several men firing at the same time will willingly and unwillingly fire collectively, less tightly perhaps than on the range, but obeying as a whole the same laws.

Here again, the effectiveness of the fire will depend almost exclusively on the more or less exact way in which the shooting is regulated: evaluation of the distance, choice of the right elevation, precise indication of the point to aim at.

A troop, in short, is a shooting machine composed of a certain number of guns.

It is well admitted that in combat, each gun will have a little wobble. The machine however will function according to the same laws and the grouping of a collective shooting on the battlefield will be the same as the one that would have been obtained with the same men on the polygon; but, so to speak, seen with a magnifying glass and magnified all the more as the emotion of the shooters will increase.

Although this theory is already very shaky, it must be examined.

We seem to have lost sight of the fact that a troop is not a meeting of guns, but a meeting of men with guns. This distinction is not negligible.

The whole theory of collective shooting rests on the postulate that each shooter applies the rules of shooting (arrange the indicated sights, take the sighting league, direct it at least summarily on the indicated objective); the shots coming from men who omit one or more of these rules are said to be "abnormal"; they are ignored.

Under the usual conditions of training of our soldiers as they are brought to the shooting ranges, the proportion of men applying the rules of shooting and the way they apply these rules present a certain regularity. It has been found that this regularity allows to predict, at least approximately, and to represent by a mathematical formula the results of the shooting of a certain number of men on the range; that is all. The "laws of collective shooting" have therefore nothing mysterious nor transcendent; they are the consequence and, one could say, the simple observation of the regularity with which our soldiers apply the rules that we taught them. For these laws to be verified in all circumstances and for one to be entitled to transpose the results of the polygon on the battlefield (by simply acting on one of the "variables" of the formula, from the lagoon to the dimensions of the grouping without modifying its shape, It is therefore necessary and sufficient that the men apply the rules of fire, if not with the same precision, at least with the same regularity as in peacetime, since this regularity is the very condition of application of a mathematical rule.

Is this so? Man's organism is deeply affected in combat. At

each moment, his physiological or psycho-physical state, to speak the language of the day, is conditioned by the reaction of external and multiple causes on his physical and psychic faculties. The laws which govern these phenomena are known to us only in a general and somewhat remote way. One fact however is beyond doubt: the same causes do not provoke in all men the same reactions nor even comparable reactions between them.

In the presence of circumstances capable of impressing him violently, a man will react in a way that is personal to him. The soldiers in combat will thus be "modified" each one with a variable intensity and sometimes in a different direction, and the number of those who, being no longer in a state to apply the rules of shooting, will produce abnormal blows, will vary at each moment in a proportion impossible to foresee. This number will sometimes grow until it includes all the shooters.

It is therefore certain that the mathematical laws of collective shooting, – laws based only on regularity in the application of certain learned rules, – are not applicable to combat, since the only theoretical affirmation that is certainly allowed to us is precisely that there will be no more regularity.

Let's move on to experience. The careful study of the facts and the concordant testimonies of those who have seen prove that on the battlefield things do not happen as we have too often supposed.

Far from finding, as one should, a unique and notable grouping – although very enlightened – at a distance of increase, one observes a dispersion not only enormous but absolutely irregular. The bullets produce on the ground the effect of a gigantic sweep or harrow from the place occupied by the shooters to the extreme ranges of the weapon, with denser parts, groupings which appear accidental and occur most often far beyond the distance of rise. – It is a rain which covers a considerable extent of ground and is momentarily transformed into a deluge on certain points.

But if, from the quite incoherent general aspect of the distribution of the blows on the battlefield, we pass to the observation of the effects, we will be forced to recognize that the will of the man manifests itself there unquestionably.

We see at every moment troops wanting, at certain chosen

moments, to crush the enemy with their fire and succeeding. We must therefore necessarily conclude that, if there are no laws of collective shooting or, more exactly, if these laws are special to polygon shooting, there are certainly means to shoot effectively and to reach the objective other than by chance.

It is the search for these means that we must undertake.

And first of all, under what conditions are the "groupings" observed on the battlefield formed?

If all the shooters were sufficiently affected morally and physically so that none of them applied the rules of firing, no desired grouping would occur; the firing, scattered over immense spaces, would only form (probably very far away) accidental, irregular, somewhat sporadic groupings that are more or less independent of the shooters' will.

This is the case for the shooting of surprised or completely demoralized troops, which has been called "panic shooting." Without going to this extreme, it often happens that a high proportion of the shooters approach it and this is what gives the fire on the battlefield its general chaotic aspect.

When in the midst of this disorderly turmoil, groupings are formed, zones of greater density at distance or longer, so that the fire becomes effective and reaches the chosen objective, these groupings are produced exclusively by the combatants still capable of applying the rules of fire. The number of shooters contributing to the effectiveness of the fire will be all the greater as there will be more brave and well-trained men in the ranks and as, in addition, the application of the rules of fire will require less attention from them.

It is indisputable that it would be advantageous, in spite of everything, to conduct the fire. This would not make effective the shooting of the producers of abnormal shots - very numerous sometimes, let us agree - but at least those who are in a position to apply the rules would shoot exactly where it is necessary.

Unfortunately, our fire control procedures are, in the normal circumstances of offensive combat, most often inapplicable.

The officer, the fire chief, assuming that he retains enough presence of mind to appreciate the elements of the fire in a sound manner, will he have the time to make the meticulous observations that he is asked to make, absorbed as he is by his role as conductor of men and coach?

He will not have too much strength to solve at every moment the difficult problems whose immediate solution is a question of life or death: to use the ground by choosing the paths, the shelters, the shooting positions; to encourage and push his men; to supervise the fight and determine the moment of the forward movements; to make open and cease the fire.

Would he usually be in a position to transmit precise indications?

Most often lying in the middle of his men or huddled behind the same shelter, in the tumult of the fight, he will have to limit his intervention to very simple orders repeated from near to near; such as: Forward, start it, hide, such direction.

Even though the leader could determine and make hear the indications necessary to the conduct of the fire, the soldier will apply them only in a very restricted measure, variable with his moral state and the more or less deep impression that the training will have made on him. Under fire, his faculty of attention will be reduced to very little and his state of over-excitement or agitation will make it physically impossible for him to make any precise and complicated movement. He will therefore accomplish the movements acquired through training all the better if he has been trained with more care, but everything that requires attention or precision known to him to change his elevation or to aim precisely at the point indicated to him, will disappear quite quickly.

This fact that the shot will usually be only partially conducted and often not at all has, from the point of view of vulnerability, notable consequences.

A man under fire always has the impression, as vivid as it is unreasonable, that he is specially and personally targeted – that he is being blamed. This is the logical reaction of the sensation of danger on an organism deprived of the faculty to reason. The observation is well known and proven by experience. Under the influence of this haunting, so that the enemy does not kill him, the human being tries to kill and it is one of the most powerful engines of the combatant.

As a result, he will shoot at the people he believes are shooting at him, i.e. at those he sees most clearly in front of him, no matter what happens. This conviction that it is these and not others who threaten him, being the direct consequence of a series of unreasoned impulses, will present itself in the form of an obviousness. The man himself will not choose his objective; this objective will impose itself.

We can see how unreasonable it would be to count on always being able to direct his shot at will to the point we have chosen.

So, no more fireworks, no more sheaves driven to their destination by means of skilfully indicated landmarks; no more targets judiciously partitioned according to their vulnerability nor artificial fire concentration. The combatant placed in the difficult conditions that we know will shoot without malice at what he sees best, at what strikes his attention. If he sees poorly or nothing, he will shoot at random.

Visibility in these conditions becomes the almost sole factor of vulnerability. All our efforts must therefore be directed toward reducing visibility, toward not attracting the attention of the enemy shooter.

To present numerous small groups moving easily and making good use of the terrain, rapid and irregular movements, men lying down whenever they are not, completely sheltered, that is what matters. As for the fact, for these small packs, of walking or stationing in long or wide, with wide or tight intervals, that is quite secondary.

If they are large pack (dense rows or columns) the question of their vulnerability is quite simple. No matter how detailed their arrangement, they will not show themselves under fire from an un-demoralized enemy.

The placement of the elements in relation to each other has no special virtue; it is the flexibility of the whole to move on the ground, the rapidity and irregularity of the movements of small groups that are easy to handle that can henceforth assure the troops, on the battlefield, a relative immunity. – It is necessary to pass unnoticed, not to attract attention; everything is there. Modesty suits the infantryman.

It should be noted that this way of looking at the question of vulnerability is absolutely consistent with the impression of witnesses of the last wars.

We can now draw from the above the following consequences:

1. The conduct of fire, in order to have a chance of being usefully exercised in combat, must be very simple and aim only at the necessary and possible things. It tends to merge with the conduct of the troop;

2. The indications of the chief will reach, whatever happens, only the men in good moral condition. These indications, moreover, can only improve the shooting of individually well-trained men. It does not matter if a man who does not aim or aims badly uses one raise rather than another. It follows that the technical conduct of the shooting is only a mediocre part of the efficiency. The conduct of the troop with a view to safeguarding its morale and the individual training of the shooter take first place, even in guided shooting;

3. The conduct of fire will very often be totally or partially lacking. It is therefore necessary that the man be able to shoot usefully without being led.

§2 – Practical Implications

1. Conduct and discipline of fire

The officer does not "conduct" the fire and even less "regulates" it; he commands men who shoot. The effectiveness of the fire depends at a given moment on the value of each of these men as a soldier and as a shooter.

Everything that the leader does to safeguard the morale of the soldier or to exalt his energy and to help the shooter will therefore contribute very actively to the effectiveness of the fire. His action, although not that of the gunner, will not be less necessary nor less important.

Almost always this action will be executed not by the precise indication of the elements of the shooting, but by indirect means: skill in leading the routes, judicious choice of the shooting positions, character and composure inspiring confidence to his troop.

Of course, whenever he can and when his men will be able to take advantage of it, the officer will give all the indications, all the advices likely to improve the shooting: distance, information on the places occupied by the enemy, attention drawn on the troops which show themselves, etc...

There remains the question of fire discipline. We have been forced to capitulate on almost all points and to recognize that usually the officer will not lead the fire, as we currently understand it: he will lead his men in such a way as to put them in the best possible conditions to shoot. Will we also have to give up the choice of when to shoot and give up any control over the consumption of ammunition?

On the contrary, let us affirm the absolute necessity for the leader to keep the disposition of his fire; he must remain master of having the fire fired and of having it cease at the appropriate moment, because otherwise it is no longer only the conduct of the fire but that of the combat which escapes him.

How to obtain the discipline of fire? Can we, without inconsistency, after what we have said, decree that the officer will have the material possibility and the authority to open and cease fire at his command?

On the contrary, we must admit that we will never prevent a man exposed to fire from firing when he sees his enemy and believes he can hit him. To let the officers believe that they can, by virtue of a simple command, obtain it in combat is therefore as dangerous as it is unreasonable, because it would dispense them from seeking the practical means to be used to open and cease fire when it is necessary.

Two aspects of fire discipline may be considered.

1. Individual discipline – the most important – aimed especially at the very numerous cases of non-conducted or incompletely conducted fire and having as its goal to prevent as much as possible the waste of ammunition.

Its basis is the following: "The man must always shoot with the

intention of reaching, on his own account, the goal he aims at."
This principle translates into a few simple rules:
One should never shoot when one cannot see.
One shoots only when there is a chance to hit.
One shoots all the more carefully, and consequently more slowly, that the goal is more difficult to reach.

These notions can only be acquired by a very serious training and very neglected until now. This training requires a lot of time and care; it requires quite profound modifications in our habits of instruction and conduct of fire in peacetime.

2. Collective discipline – which relies almost entirely on indirect means and is much more a matter of troop leadership than fire leadership.

One should only ask for things that are possible; it is to encourage indiscipline to teach a man in peacetime what one knows cannot be done in combat.

We will therefore admit the following principles: when a man receives rifle fire, he will only be prevented from firing at the enemy he sees by placing him in such a situation that he cannot fire, or at least by keeping him in a formation that makes firing difficult. The only way to stop the fire (unless the enemy stops his own) is to make the shooters disappear behind cover, thus exploiting the instinct for self-preservation, or sometimes, if morale is sufficient, by provoking a leap forward.

Practically, since the rapid-fire and long-range rifles, this is how fire discipline has always been sought and often obtained in war. The preoccupation to show one's men and to put them in a position to fire only at the very moment of opening fire is in perfect harmony with the other conditions of combat and will not create any new difficulty in practice.

The consequences of these principles for the training of men and cadres are easy to deduce and everyone can formulate them.

It is all the more important to specify them since almost all the questions concerning infantry firing in combat are strictly dependent on the discipline of fire.

The "speed" of fire is an example. The infantry having a rapid-fire weapon is not made to fire slowly. Our efforts must therefore tend to make it fire quickly, but by intermittent periodicals, and this requires first of all that we can open and cease fire at will. The nature of the means to be used to obtain this allows us to notice that if the infantryman must be trained to use more and more intermittent fire, it is not necessary to try to make him do sudden bursts of fire and suddenly extinguished like those of the gun. The bursts of the rifle can only be short periods of individual fire executed always with as much care as the circumstances will allow, the fire usually lighting up and above all extinguishing itself progressively and gradually.

2. Training of the troop

The effectiveness of a shot depends above all on the quality of each shooter at the moment considered.

We have seen the officer transform himself little by little from a fireman to a man driver. His main role is to put the soldier in a good position to shoot, in particular to support his morale.

It is the bravest who shoot the best because they are less affected physically and morally by the emotions of combat.

As for the shooter, we will be guided in his preparation by this principle: there is no collective shooting. In combat, there are men who simultaneously shoot individually. These men can be helped in some cases by the leader, who indicates to each of them the elements of the shot; other times they will have to act without direction.

There is thus strictly speaking only one instruction of shooting, the individual instruction. The collective instruction is almost entirely negative; it consists in teaching the men to shoot in a group without losing the habits they have acquired in individual shooting.

It remains to determine the basis of individual training. We want to train combat shooters, that is to say, men capable, not of shooting with precision at the range, but of shooting usefully in the special conditions indicated previously – that is to say, of reaching with the minimum of attention and fatigue a goal analogous to those which are presented in combat.

It follows that our instruction must be almost entirely training; its purpose will be to make our men acquire – by a long repetition

of the same exercises – "habits":
- Habits of body (physical training);
- Habits of mind (tactical training).

Let us notice in particular that if one generally admits the utility of the daily and relatively prolonged sessions of setting in cheek and aiming, the importance of the education of the eye does not seem yet enough recognized. It is one of the most notable lessons of recent wars that we must shoot far away on objectives that are not very visible.

We must train our men to see well. Most of them – for lack of exercise – do not distinguish at practical combat distances; this must be the subject of a very long and rather difficult to organize training.

There is no doubt that the man in combat will shoot quickly; if he is only taught to shoot slowly, he will shoot at random. We must make speed of fire a regular part of our training.

Experience shows that almost always on the battlefield the shot is too high. We must try to fight this tendency by training tricks such as: always aiming at low goals, at ground level, and requiring that in the movement of "cheek" the weapon arrives at the shoulder with the barrel slightly inclined below the horizontal.

The tactical training of the shooter is still almost unknown in our country, and it is one of the most deplorable consequences of the theory of collective shooting, which knew only the "man-gun" automatically executing the order of the chief. It is indeed a question, let us note it, of training, i.e. of habits to be taken by the very frequent application of some simple rules and not of knowledge to be acquired.

The principle of tactical training, already mentioned, can be formulated as follows: in all circumstances, a man must shoot with the firm intention of reaching, on his own behalf, the goal he is aiming at. One shoots only when there is a probability of reaching the goal.

It is an instruction to be organized; it requires a lot of care and includes the following subjects:

The research of objectives through the campaign;

The estimation of the probability of hitting according to the distance, visibility, size or movement of the target;

The habit of never firing when not seen and of ceasing fire without command when the enemy disappears;

The habit of firing when necessary without the help of the leader; this implies the choice of the objective and the distribution of the fire.

There is no question of the choice of the elevator; the unleaded man will always shoot with the combat elevator.

Let us observe in conclusion that the best training would still be to shoot often. The daily frequentation of the weapon, the education of the eye, this slow appropriation of the organism, result of a long practice, are unfortunately hardly compatible with the social conditions where we live. At least we must try to take advantage of the short passage of the men under the flags by judiciously using the allocated cartridges, and to develop the practice of shooting in the nation.

§3 – Use of Fire

This excursion into the field of fire will allow us to summarize briefly the principles which should guide the initiative of officers in the solution of the multiple problems of the use of fire.

Two points are to be considered:

How can we shoot?

For what purpose do we want to fire?

Sometimes one will be able to command one's troop as on the range, while in other circumstances it will escape all control and direction.

It would be as unreasonable to consider this complete anarchy as the general case as it would be to expect to always regulate the shooting and conduct it by procedures similar to those we employ in peacetime.

In the usual circumstances of combat, the leader can and must direct the fire of his men. But it will not be enough for him, as one seems to believe, to indicate the elements of the fire, to fix an objective, to order the opening of fire or its extinction. His role is more difficult and it is not with a simple command that he can flatter himself to fulfill it.

It is only thanks to the judicious use of indirect means appropriate to the circumstances that he will succeed in using the fire of his men at the desired moment and for a determined purpose. It is thus important for him above all to know exactly to what extent and in what form his will can intervene in the execution of the fire.

We have tried to show that if sometimes this will can be imposed as completely and as directly as in peacetime, most often it will be necessary to be satisfied with a more summary and somewhat more distant action.

At effective combat distances, when it is a question, under fire, of employing the fire of his troop, the officer will have to reckon with our previous observations:

The man will no longer modify his rise and will shoot at the objective that he sees best in front of him; it will be very difficult to make him change his objective.

He will shoot quickly and most often by using the repetition, because "it is more convenient." The intensity of the fire will thus hardly vary, especially in the offensive, with the number of men in line and, if the man is well trained, with the difficulty of reaching the goal.

As soon as one puts him in a position to shoot, the combatant, if he receives bullets, will necessarily shoot. Unless there is a very noticeable lull, the only way to stop firing is to shelter the shooters or to change places.

The conclusion that must be drawn is this. Apart from circumstances, exceptional in fact, where the leader can directly direct the fire, one must not count on a skilfully nuanced fire, opened and ceased at the precise minute that one has chosen. No artificial concentrations of fire or changes of objectives obtained at will; no shooters with their finger on the trigger, waiting for a sign to "unleash the burst" as we say today.

The officer commanded men whose firing capacity and resistance to demoralization he knew from experience; it was a matter of spending them wisely in view of the desired result and of making them produce as much as possible. To support their morale, to choose their firing position in front of the objective that one wants to reach, to keep them hidden until the opening of fire, to make them appear at the right moment, to draw their attention to the enemy troops who show up, to withdraw them from the fire when one wants them not to fire any more, this is what the action of the leader on the fire will most often be limited to.

Whatever the expected result of the fire (to advance, to wear down the enemy, to gain time by delaying him...), the immediate goal will always be to act on him by frightening him, by demoralizing him more or less. But a slow and parsimonious fire, even prolonged, is incapable of producing this necessary impression. It is therefore ineffective and it must be a principle for us never to use a slow fire that we know is worthless.

Our rule will be to fire only when the fire can be effective and to employ then enough means to obtain as quickly as possible the desired result. As soon as this result is reached or is recognized as momentarily impossible, all our efforts must be directed not to restrict but to cease firing.

The practice is difficult. A lively fire cannot be sustained and should take the form of short bursts separated by periods of rest.

Unfortunately, we can only rely on a rough discipline of fire. The fireworks that are proposed to us for this purpose... all have some advantages, so it is advisable not to neglect any of them. But none is of a certain effectiveness in all the cases.

The result is that all our efforts will often be powerless to produce this succession of short bursts separated by complete silence. We will then have to limit our ambition to open fire by deploying our men, only at the moment of need and, when this fire becomes useless, to provoke its more or less complete and fast extinction by making the shooters hide or move.

Long distance fire is powerless to obtain "decisive" results. This is a fact of experience, for which several reasons can be cited; the main one is that fire will always be insufficient to completely neutralize a solid troop if it is not combined with the fear of boarding. The fire alone can be combined with the forward movement immediately threatening for the enemy.

Fires should therefore be used at large and medium distances (beyond 800 meters, for example), when one wishes to avoid or delay a decision; this is a maneuver.

If, instead of avoiding the decision, or looking for it, it is always at the effective distances of combat (below Boo meters to fix the ideas) that one will make it mature.

In the offensive you only shoot to advance. The immediate goal is to demoralize the defender so that he fires badly or no longer fires. We know that the omission of fire always slows down the forward march. Firing from a distance, moreover, on sheltered men will produce only insignificant results. At all distances, a parsimonious and slow fire is without effect.

It follows that one will fire only when it has become impossible to advance without having acted on the enemy. But then one will immediately use as many rifles as the terrain will allow, or at least a number deemed to be largely sufficient. From the beginning, one must ensure a superiority all the more marked as one wants to advance more quickly.

The application of these principles is not without presenting in practice some difficulties and the question deserves a thorough study; we will limit ourselves here to some remarks.

1. This observation of the uselessness of an insufficient fire and this principle, that it is desirable in the offensive to speak fire as late as possible but with a great superiority of means, do not change anything to the necessity of directing the combat, of deploying only at the right time and of conserving people to feed the line of combat.

The art consists in taking into account these different factors to a degree that varies with the circumstances and that it is impossible to evaluate theoretically: "it is an art of execution."

2. From the fact that distant fire is rarely useful, it does not follow that the closest fire will always be the best. It will often happen, on the contrary, that a firing position at 800 meters, for example, will be much more advantageous than others closer at 600 or 500 meters.

It is the occupants of the good firing positions, momentarily stopped, who will protect the other fractions with their fire and will allow them to gain ground until we have found better.

3. We have stated that in the offensive we shoot to advance. Will it not often happen, on the contrary, that the frontal attack will fire only to occupy the enemy while he is being turned, like the British in the second period of the Transvaal campaign?

This would be a very dangerous conception.

Understood in this way, a demonstration has no value.

In an offensive action, everyone must attack with the intention of succeeding. If on certain points an attack turns into a "demonstration," it is because the terrain will oppose its march or because the commander will not have given it sufficient means. – The commander of a troop must never leave with the intention of not arriving. To fix the enemy, to convince him that we are seriously attacking, it is essential to believe it yourself.

Conclusions

In conclusion, let us content ourselves with summarizing very briefly the main ideas which we feel are likely to guide the reflections and direct the efforts of the infantry officer in his task as educator.

Today, as in the past, the offensive combat of the infantry is defined in one word: advance. But to advance in front of today's weapons would be mostly impossible with the old methods. The rapidity of the fire produces a considerable moral effect, and its great range increases disproportionately the time during which the combatant would have to undergo an ordeal too strong for his body.

To reduce this ordeal, the attack has two means:

Exploiting the terrain in order to evade the effects of the enemy's fire;

To make a superior fire to extinguish or at least attenuate that of the adversary.

All the technique of our training will thus aim at two results: the flexibility of the formations and the effectiveness of the fire.

The real difficulty of our peacetime task results from the obligation, if we want to do a useful job, to subordinate the technical elements to the psychic elements, which are much more delicate to determine and which it is impossible to experience directly.

The fact, for example, of avoiding material losses is only a means, and the goal of the use of the ground is to bring to a good distance men physically and morally capable of fighting. The formations most likely to avoid losses may not, therefore, be the most advantageous in all circumstances of combat.

This concern to take into account the moral conditions of combat is nowhere more necessary than in the question of fire.

On the whole, the conduct of combat has changed little. The most notable and characteristic change is this: the terrain asserts itself in all circumstances as an indispensable and often tyrannical collaborator of the leader whose task is complicated by this dependence. The value of formations and methods of marching is measured by the facilities they provide for using the terrain, and the role of senior officers in combat is almost limited to estimating the quantity of men that will have to be expended to obtain a given result, and to bringing these men to the desired point and time, in good physical and moral shape.

For the rest, the experience of recent war events, far from shaking the known principles of combat, only confirms them.

In front of the infantry rifle, the consumption of men is enormous, not because of material losses, whose number would tend to decrease, but because of the very rapid wear and tear of a troop under fire. An attack, to be powerful, must therefore involve a series of successive efforts, and, consequently, a profound procedure.

A maneuver – distant fire, approaches and night combat, attempted investment – is often necessary but never sufficient in the face of a solid enemy; it prepares and facilitates combat but does not replace it.

It is always necessary to come, on certain points at least, to the direct attack and pushed to the limit. This final crisis seems, in cold blood, purely impossible. No tactical procedure, no training can explain it. It is a matter of morale, and the goal of our tactical efforts will be especially to prepare this solution and to make it possible, by opposing closely morally superior troops to an adversary depressed by the conscience of its inferiority and paralyzed by the fire.

Success depends, in the end, on the fighting ability of the troops; judicious training and skill in tactical procedures are important, but something else is needed. Moral superiority in the special form of the offensive spirit is the sign of those who will win, the last soldier must be marked by it known the leader. This observation has important consequences.

We are sometimes led to believe that, thanks to the perfection of weapons and the strength of resistance that the defensive can acquire, the supreme art in battle will be to vary at will the attitude of one's troops and to give them in certain points a defensive mission in order to attack more advantageously on other points.

This is a dangerous conception. It is not possible to measure or nuance this moral breath which is the offensive spirit, and in an army worthy of victory, when a fraction in combat, however small, does not advance, it is by force. It sometimes stops, but, like the water of a torrent before a dam, beating the obstacle and pressing it with all the energy of its living force.

Our infantry combat, contrary to some common ideas, has become, in its essential lines, simpler. The task of the commander is more and more limited to judiciously equipping his troops, and his intervention, all of foresight, in order to be less complicated in its form, only becomes heavier.

Precise orders for immediate execution, the meticulous distribution of work, the permanent liaison of movements in the course of action no longer have their place in our engagements and it is in this sense that we have been able to affirm that success depends largely on the value of the troop. From the moment it is "decoupled," a combat unit has only two elements to condition its action:

One material : an objective to reach;

The other moral: the will to reach this objective.

And as the splitting into numerous autonomous groups becomes the rule of our movements on the battlefield, the convergence and the coordination of efforts can no longer be ensured, in an offensive action of today, only under two conditions: a troop must always march on a determined objective known to all and no longer serve as a satellite to another unit only aware of the direction desired by the leader. Thus assured in its direction, it still needs, to fulfill its mission, an independent motor; this will be the will to reach at all costs the designated objective, that is to say the offensive spirit which must permanently animate the last man.

These ideas are only observations and it must be so; a combat doctrine can only be based on facts enlightened by common sense.

If we study the most powerful tools of war of modern times, such as the armies of France at the beginning of the nineteenth century or those of Germany in 1870, we will always find this character common to all victorious armies: a total offensive spirit without ulterior motive animating, to the same degree, leaders and soldiers.

We can now join the Japanese armies of today and, without fear of error, formulate the true cause of their extraordinary successes in the face of an exceptionally solid adversary. It is not the superiority of their tactics nor the science learned in our military schools in Europe that we will have to ask the Japanese for in order to win, it is their admirable offensive spirit.

Part Two: Training and Instruction of the Troop

If it is certainly possible to find in the study of modern offensive combat a solid base and a reasonable orientation for the instruction of the troop, the passage to practice is not without difficulties.

In addition to the regulations which constitute the "letter" of the training, there are the habits and traditions which determine its "spirit." It is these habits that are most important to change, and this requires a long effort.

For three years, in the command of an infantry battalion, we have been researching and experimenting with ways to make the lessons of recent wars practically usable for infantry training. In order to keep track of these tests and in order to guide the instructors in their daily task, as soon as a question seemed to be ripe, we summed it up in a "booklet" intended for the officers of the battalion.

It is these "booklets" that will be found in the second part of this work. Although they are far from complete and have many gaps, we give them in the form in which they were "practiced"; preferring not to mature – by trying to fill in these gaps – unverified ideas with materials from experience.

These notes are not, therefore, theoretical speculations but absolutely practical advice on methods of instruction and training which have been studied in the field in collaboration with the troops, and which have in part already borne fruit.

30th INFANTRY REGIMENT
1st Battalion
Summary of theories

Booklet 1– Training and Instruction of the Young Soldier

Contents

There is an urgent need to improve and simplify our methods of training the troops.

The Regulations have made our task easier by eliminating unnecessary movements; those that are retained are not all of equal importance and we should take advantage of the initiative left to us to direct our efforts towards "the most useful."

In the training of the troop for today's combat, the "necessary" is increasingly summarized in two points:

1. Solid individual training reduced to a small number of movements, but very thorough in the sounds of the development and softening of the man and the practice of shooting;

2. Collective training and softening of the group (section or half-section) in varied terrain.

It is thus on these two points that our efforts must be concentrated, by decreasing, if it is necessary, the time devoted to the collective exercises with tight rows on the place of exercise which must definitively pass to the second rank.

Our training methods, as they are applied, do not meet our new needs. Only gymnastics instruction& is making some progress in a reasonable direction.

The purpose of this note is to indicate to the instructors the orientation that it seems useful to give to their work. We examine the following points:

I. Individual training of the man;

2. The notion of "direction" replacing the old idea of "alignment";

3. Training of the group;

4. Teaching the first elements of field service;

5. Tactical training of the troop;

6. Organization of training and use of time.

N.B. – The softening up of the section and the company for combat and the training of the gunner are treated separately in the following booklets.

I – Individual training of the man

At the same time training and training, individual instruction does not have for ideals – as one seems to believe too often - to cast all our men in the same mold, to crystallize them under an average and regular form.

Its aim must be to develop them individually in order to obtain from each one of them the maximum efficiency of which he is susceptible in the execution of the movements useful to war. We will not lose any more a precious and parsimoniously measured time, in the search of identical executions and exact cadences.

Our present method of making imitation of a gesture the principal and almost the only method of instruction is rudimentary. It gives mediocre results and causes a considerable loss of time.

We must get out of the habit of considering the movements ordered and described in their external form in the Rules as rites with a virtue of their own.

The Rules set out in detail how to perform certain movements, for two reasons:

To obtain the regularity and uniformity necessary so that the men in the line do not interfere with each other;

To indicate the procedures that experience has shown to be the most advantageous for obtaining a given result.

It is the result to be obtained, i.e. the goal of each movement, that must first be known and understood by the men.

Then they should be shown progressively and methodically the appropriate means to obtain this result, and care should be taken not to correct a fault directly at the beginning by a reminder of the rules, as we almost always do.[*]

In order to bring a man to correct himself, it is usually sufficient to make him realize that he will more easily obtain the desired result by acting differently.

It is only when he has understood and performed correctly several times that we can rectify an error, caused by an oversight or lack of attention, by a simple warning which will then awaken a precise idea in him. It should be noted, moreover, that the main task of the instructor consists much less in the *explanation* of the movements than in the *rectification* of the young soldiers' attempts. It is therefore necessary to teach him above all to rectify judiciously.

As a young corporal cannot be expected to have sufficient experience to find out for himself the procedures to be used in each particular case, it is the *officer* who must teach him these procedures, and see that he complies with them.

The application of this method requires that instructors have a much more complete and thoughtful knowledge of what they are to teach.

In practice, it will be necessary, for the elements, to renounce

---

[*] It should be noted that a certain number of movements serve only to prepare for another, and it is only by executing this second movement that the soldier will be able to determine whether he has executed the previous one well. For example, the position "a genou" has no other result than an easy pointing. it is impossible to know if one is well placed other than by pointing. similarly, since "la garde" is only designed to prepare for the execution of bayonet fencing movements such as "Un pas en avent" or "Pointez," the man can only rectify himself by verifying if he has executed these movements easily. It will be necessary to give up the habit of excessive breaking down and to pass to the next movement only when the previous one is correct. In particular, certain movements that could be called "preparatory" will be taught only summarily and without trying to perfect them before moving on to the useful movement they are preparing.

almost entirely to collective instruction. The instructors will spend their time at the beginning taking each man in turn; five minutes of "private instruction" is more profitable than half an hour of poorly supervised exercise. This will lead to new habits, such as watching the instructors less and checking their results more carefully.

To make clear in what spirit the problems of individual training should be approached, we shall briefly review the principal balances of the body described in the Regulations:

A. Position of the soldier in the line with or without arms.

B. Position of the charge and crossing the bayonet.

C. Bayonet fencing guard.

A – Position of the soldier in the line

The purpose is to obtain a relatively stable balance of the standing body, intended to last a short time, without the man having to present special resistance in any given direction; the body holding as little space as possible and ready to immediately execute certain movements of arms and legs requiring little effort.

It follows that the body must be upright (shoulders at the same height, feet equally open), resting not on the heels - which, with the legs together and stretched out, is a tiring position, not very stable and not allowing instantaneous movement – but on the soles of the feet, with the heels touching the ground without pressure.

This requires the body to be leaning forward significantly.

Remarks. – It is quite difficult to get the upper body to be sufficiently forward, that the feet are equally open.

It should be made clear to the men that "tucking in the belt" is the same as bending forward; they should see that they are less fatigued and can start easily in this position.

In order to obtain symmetrical opening of the feet, it is necessary that the position of the man be determined; in practice, it is almost never determined, because one omits to indicate what one must face.

In individual training and for all movements, never forget to indicate to the man a point to which he must face; vary this point, cause the correct placement of the feet by instructing the soldier to look successively at his feet and at the point of direction (this is the first application of the notion of "direction or orientation" discussed below).

Except for a few badly balanced men, for whom special flexibility will be needed, it is quite easy to get the shoulders to be at the same height, provided that they are taken care of. This balance of the body on the two hips is more difficult to obtain in movements with the weapon; it will be the object of special attention. The position of the soldier in the line will be quickly and well taken provided that the ranks teach it properly and take advantage of all the opportunities that arise to have their men placed correctly (theories, reviews in the rooms, calls, gatherings). It is extremely important that in his corrections the instructor always operates in the same order, according to a well determined method.

In this movement, he will verify, for example:

1. If the man is facing the point indicated, with his feet equally open;

2. If the body is well projected forward, the head direct;

3. If the body is plumb on the hips, the shoulders at the same height;

4. Details: left hand, weapon if any, etc...

B – Position of the charge and crossing the bayonet

The aim is twofold:

1. It is a question of obtaining a position of equilibrium upright as stable and little fatigued as possible; what would correspond to the body balanced on the two hips, the legs light and open, the distance between the feet being approximately equal to their length; the center of gravity being projected in front, between the feet;

2. But the man must in addition offer a sufficient resistance it an effort of front in back and to be able to put in play easily. It will thus be necessary obliquely so as to have a point of support behind while remaining able to present the right shoulder to the stick.

Remarks. – One should first try to obtain a well balanced position on both legs, without fatigue or stiffness.

The man will not take it the first time with a sudden

movement, but by tapping, and then will gradually get used to the position without hesitation.

For the obliquity of the lunge and the inclination of the body forward, one will obtain it by making note of the disadvantages of the committed faults.

If the fencer is not sufficiently slanted backwards or does not have his upper body sufficiently forward, show him that he is not solid by making an effort from front to back on his weapon; if he is not sufficiently straight, have him put him at gunpoint. In all cases, let him rectify himself. Never omit to indicate the point to which one must face, which eliminates the very common fault of placing the weapon obliquely and not perpendicularly to the rank.

C – Bayonet fencing guard.

It is an unstable balance and on "tension" intended to prepare certain fast and violent movements.

It is necessary to obtain :

1. The balance; the body bearing equally on the two legs slightly bent, the bust straight, the arms free.

Experience shows that this is quite difficult. The body usually rests on the right hip, and the right hand rests the weapon on the thigh. This defective position usually results from leaving the men on guard for too long, which should be avoided with the greatest care.

This balance will be taught first without weapons, and each man will practice taking the guard a large number of times in a row, but will remain there each time only for a very short time;

2. The tension, that is to say a position forming a spring and allowing a sudden effort in the form of a trigger.

It is the placement of the legs that matters; it cannot be the same for all men.

A man can only be brought to his proper guard by having certain elementary movements ("Step forward or backward"; "Point") performed and repeated a fair number of times.

One then sees the guard changing and tending to settle in a position that will most often be good, and the right hand no longer resting on the thigh. If the man does not manage to do this on his own, we suggest that he try certain modifications (more or less split, etc.) and we show him that his movements become easier.

The guard, it should not be forgotten, is a preparatory movement that must be shown first summarily and to the extent necessary to pass to the movements n' islands whose more or less easy and correct execution will alone allow to verify if the position is good and to rectify judiciously this position.

Let us note in this respect that bayonet fencing is an individual gymnastics; one will thus avoid with the greatest care to seek "the whole." It is not a question of teaching the men the correct execution, at a determined rhythm, of strictly regular movements – as in the old "handling of weapons" – but of exercising them with the aim of easing them to execute often with an increasing vigor certain useful movements. The learning of the "Pointez:" movement, for example, which is very easy to learn, has no value in itself. What is important is to train the soldier to point very often, making an effort to increase the rapidity and vigor of the trigger and the lengthening of the lunge.

II – Notion of "direction."

Our methods of marching in view of combat and in combat are necessarily modified. As soon as a unit is no longer marching in mass and absolutely under cover, any rigid system in which the movement of each element is determined by an interval and a distance to be kept in relation to a unit of direction becomes impracticable.

The imperative need to use the terrain, the fragmentation into numerous elements and the extent of the marching fronts require that each group have a large degree of independence, and the whole movement can only be coordinated by a common direction.

In our exercises we find it more convenient to keep our companies or sections on a leash and to move them like pawns on a chessboard. It is necessary to give up these habits which are more and more inapplicable in the modern combat.

Both in the approaches and during the battle, a group, whatever it may be, must never move without having an objective in a predetermined direction, and the march thus becomes, for any fraction, large or small, a series of jumps from one point of the terrain to another point as exactly defined as possible.

The application certainly suffers from some difficulties, especially because this dominant preoccupation with orientation does not accord with the principles on which our instruction has so long rested.

It is therefore important to modify our morals by giving little by little in all our methods of instruction a preponderant place to the notion of "direction."

The consequences of this change are many and deserve serious consideration.

The procedures used to order our marches and rallies were based, until recently, and are even partly based on two geometric principles:

Alignment, i.e. the act of placing or maintaining oneself in the prolongation of a line determined by a certain number of points;

The notion of the perpendicular. For example: to establish a column perpendicular to a front drawn in advance, in gatherings; to change direction under a fixed angle almost always right (to the right, face to the right, square movements, etc...)

The drawing of the base line (in rallies) and the orientation of the formation (in marches) are the sole responsibility of the leader through his markers or his guide.

A long habit prevents us from noticing how artificial these methods are, how impractical in varied terrain and how long they take to learn. The only argument in their favor is that, on the exercise ground, for the reviews, one can obtain more precision in the drawing of the lines, at the price of a laborious training. This argument has no more value, since necessarily the evolutions with tight rows of the maneuver field pass to the second plan.

It is a question of replacing these two principles by the following one: any movement or any gathering is determined above all by its orientation with respect to the visible points of the ground.

All our current formations and evolutions can be completely reconstructed on this principle.

Examples: A rank will be formed of men facing the same point on the horizon (far enough away so that parallelism is sufficient) and placed at the same height. This will be the new alignment.

An assembly will be formed of units each established on its own account facing a specified point, then placed at the prescribed distance and interval.

In the frontal march, each man will walk frankly and with equal step towards the fixed point, attentive only not to overtake his neighbors, etc.

The complete transformation of our habits can only be done little by little. In the meantime, the Regulations give us the means to prepare for it by directing our efforts in a direction that we know is useful.

We must take advantage of this and develop by all means the feeling of "direction" which must become the basis of our training.

From now on, while complying with the regulations, we will take advantage of the latitude granted to us under the following conditions:

Individual Instruction. – From the very beginning, the principal notion given to the man will be, not once known to "line up" with his neighbor, but to face exactly to a point indicated.

From the position of the unarmed soldier and for all the elements of individual instruction, the man will always have a direction and it will be one of his first exercises to learn to place himself correctly in front of a determined and often changing point.

In individual marching, men will no longer walk following each other on a track, but will always walk towards a point of direction. The main thing is, in fact, to obtain a direct and rectilinear walk towards the fixed point; the rest is detail.

Collective Flexibility. – Once the group of a few men is assembled, it will always gather a workbench "in front of something" and will never walk without a direction being indicated.

By choice, square movements, right or left, will be replaced by oblique movements, and the group will be trained to face all visible points on the horizon very quickly.

In evolution or flexibility exercises, deployments, changes of direction on foot or on the march should always be made facing a point on the ground.

Deployments without any indication of objective or perpendicular to the direction followed are special cases that should be deliberately neglected.

Gatherings. – Assemblies, large or small, will always be oriented in a specific direction. Each unit, after having faced the fixed point, moves to its place.

To determine the assemblies no longer by the drawing of a line marking its front, but by the point it must face, is the only practical way of orienting a troop surely and rapidly in view of an engagement or a movement.

III - Training of the group

We had to assign as main goal to the individual training not the regularity of the movements and their uniformity, but the research, for each man, of the maximum useful output. This training with an individualistic tendency must be completed by a simultaneous learning of cohesion, because cohesion alone makes the troop.

The usual conditions of combat forbid us to ask exclusively for this cohesion from the old habituation of the rank in the immediate and regular execution of a "command." We must now look for it in the habit of acting collectively in view of a common goal in a much more conscious, freer and more frequent way than before. Hence the necessity to start as early as possible the practice of useful movements.

Although it is a bit of a clash with our old customs, we must teach the young soldier, as soon as he arrives, the first elements of solidarity and collective acts, not only in the form of movements in the ranks and shoulder to shoulder, but in their practical form of very simple evolutions outside.

Man does not need to know how to shoot or put a weapon on his shoulder, nor even how to march at a pace or line up to learn, in a group of a few men, to face an indicated point, to open up, to close up, to assemble, to march across the field towards an object he sees.

Even a cursory study of modern combat shows us that the

action of the command is most often reduced to the fixing of a common goal. The lines break up into groups, each of them acting on its own in view of the goal to be reached. This elementary group, a true combat unit, must become the basis of our infantry detail tactics, and its education will be the main part of our preparation. The usual circumstances require that it be small in number; the peacetime section (20-25 men) seems suitable as a type. This will be our combat group.

In order to build up the group little by little and to begin its training, we will act as follows:

When the men have learned to face a point and to walk towards this point, that is to say a few days after their arrival, we will gather them, for this instruction, in very small groups at first (4 or 5 men). As they become more confident in their movements, the size of the groups will be gradually increased to reach the normal strength of 20-25 men (section in peacetime, half-section in war).

The training of the group is then merged with the instruction of the section and includes, at the same time as the relaxation in dispersed order (which is discussed in one of the following booklets), all the regulatory movements of the section with tight ranks.

During the first period, we will limit ourselves to a few very simple movements repeated very often on all kinds of terrain, without "looking for difficulty." It is not only a question of making the men understand these movements in such a way that they can execute them in a thoughtful manner, but of arriving at a point where, by frequent repetition, they are executed without any hesitation and in a sort of mechanical way. The training of the group for shooting will continue in parallel; this is discussed below.

The small group (progressively increased), first in one row and then in two rows, will thus be trained every day in the following movements:

1. Facing a point; assembling facing a point.

Each man faces the indicated point and then stands at the height of the man designated as the base, without any other concern for alignment and without losing sight of the point of direction. One always gathers behind the instructor, who himself faces the direction.

(Exercise to be repeated very often at the beginning of the instruction).

2. Walk to a designated point (changing this point often).

3. Spreading out with firm feet and walking (two steps and five steps).

Numerous exercises of walking towards successive points of direction by widening and tightening.

4. To deploy oneself directly in front of any point of the horizon.

This is the typical exercise for combat.

In all the marching exercises, the man does not lose sight of the point of direction, being only attentive to remain approximately at the level of the base man. When the point of direction is too close, he must be accustomed to move a little to the right or left, depending on his place in the line.

As often as possible we will work in the countryside.

IV – Teaching the elements of field service

If the "imitation" method is of little benefit for individual training in the parade ground, it is deplorable when it comes to the elements of field service such as the use of terrain, concealed marching, patrol and sentry duty. The habitual use of a process of having former soldiers perform these movements in front of recruits who must imitate them is one of the main causes of the poor results obtained.

In short, these are direct applications of the most elementary common sense. Let us address ourselves directly to common sense.

The principle will be to always propose, from the beginning, a goal to be reached, a result to be obtained without indicating the solution.

When the goal is understood, man will almost always find the means to be used; never rectify a rule by a reminder, but by a reminder of common sense and by bringing to light, as often as possible, incidents that highlight the errors committed.

Let's take an example: in the first outdoor sessions, we try to make people understand the use of the field and the role of the patrollers.

Field use. The recruits are divided into two groups. Group No. 1 is placed, as far as possible, on an elevation of the ground with a fairly wide view, in medium-converted terrain. Group No. 2 is led 600-800 meters from the first and assembled in full view, but near the first cover.

The men of the group no. 1 are installed, broken ranks, without any constraint, in order to see well. They are shown and made to adjust with their rifle the group no. 2, by prescribing them to watch their comrades and to shoot at them each time they see them.

It is explained to the men of the group no. 2 that it is a question of approaching as close as possible, without being close, to the group no. 1 to remove it. Then, without any further explanation, the ranks are broken and everyone goes his own way. '

If the location is well chosen, group no. 1 is almost always surprised by those who have made their way well; from this, one learns the necessity to watch the parts of the terrain that are not seen, by placing sentries.

The exercise was repeated several times, changing groups and on different terrains.

It is a good way to get used to the terrain and to develop initiative. It is noted that, provided that the aim is understood and that they are allowed to act freely from the first day, the young soldiers use the terrain very well.

Patrols. – Nothing is more likely to give them false ideas than to invite young soldiers to watch a patrol work, and then to have them imitate what they have seen.

Besides, these demonstration movements are always implausible, because one could not follow a well-done patrol with one's eyes.

In order to give a more accurate idea from the very first sessions, one can act as follows:

Posts are placed in advance in a certain number of hamlets, farms, woods, etc.

The Company being assembled, it is pointed out to the young soldiers that they cannot start marching until they know whether the enemy occupies such a farm or such a wood that they are shown, because they would be exposed to being shot at. The lesson is clearer by taking care to be surprised by a first post.

A certain number of groups of four or five young soldiers, without officers, are then formed and each one is told: "The idea is to go and see, without being seen, if the enemy occupies such and such a farm or wood and to find out if there are many of them"; then they are given their freedom.

The information reported is checked; it is verified whether the patrol has been seen and those who have succeeded are congratulated.

By having one or more of these improvised patrols removed, one will show them that they should not walk "in packs," etc.

These examples are given only to make the method clear. It is the task of each training officer to devise small themes and systems to highlight what he wants to teach.

He should limit his initial training exercises to the "elements" (use and knowledge of the terrain, placement and search for small posts, patrols and small reconnaissance operations towards a given goal, etc.), avoiding general exercises and especially combat exercises, which should only be started when the group's training is fairly advanced.

The main thing is to always pose the problem clearly, carefully avoiding any technical expression. It is only when he has understood and executed what we want him to do that the young soldier must learn that he has been on a "patrol," or that he has been on "sentry duty," or that he has served as a "communication man," etc.

Almost all our young soldiers will be able to do field service in this way naturally – as Mr. Jourdain spoke in prose – when they are convinced that the military is allowed to use their common sense like everyone else.

To obtain good results, no theory, no demonstration on the parade ground, concerning field service, should be given to the recruits before they are taken into the field.

V – Tactical training of the troops

Tactical training for combat is often poorly given and sometimes not given at all to lower ranks and soldiers. This is a gap that must be filled.

It is generally limited to teaching the man a few regulatory prescriptions concerning the discipline of fire, the loading of the magazine of his weapon or what he should do when his comrade in combat is wounded; moral recommendations are attached to it on the obligation to follow one's leader, not to remain behind under any pretext or to defend the flag. All this is very useful and the "duties in combat," in particular, will have to be the subject of frequent discussions illustrated with examples.

But it is not enough. Most of our men can and should rise above the training itself and have a tactical instruction, a combat "doctrine" appropriate to their situation. To have a doctrine is to have acquired the habit, given the same circumstances, of always acting in the same direction. This habit is the result of a real intellectual training that will be undertaken as soon as the man has practiced shooting, field service and the first combat exercises.

Even well-made lectures will not suffice; they leave in the mind only notions that are often vague and always without activity. The ideas, to become useful, must be assimilated little by little by frequent repetition, closely linked to practice.

The material to be taught will therefore be condensed in the form of a few rules, but as affirmative as possible, which will be repeated very often, taking advantage of every opportunity to ask men and officers about their application in combat exercises and maneuvers. Simple formulas should be sought that can be easily imprinted in the mind and used often in demonstrating their application in the field. The word retained suggests the rule and let us not forget that the tactical teaching for the lower ranks and for the soldiers must be summarized in positive rules. We will limit ourselves to indicating the basics here.

The infantryman's training must be done with a view to offensive combat; defending is an accident that is suffered as little as possible and for as long as possible. It is not at all desirable to have inferior cadres and men who are too familiar with the theory of defense; moreover, if a defensive battle must be fought, it is still with a troop trained for the offensive that one will defend oneself best.

Therefore, from the outset, defense will be considered as a momentary "stopgap" in the training of the man. This is the spirit of our rules.

Here, by way of example, is how the principles of combat can be translated into rules for the use of lower ranks and soldiers.

A - Offensive combat

1. In order to be victorious, one must frighten the enemy; when one is afraid, one is defeated. The only way to frighten the enemy is to attack him resolutely without worrying about whether you are the strongest.

2. When one encounters the enemy, one must always attack him unless one has received orders not to do so.

3. To attack is to advance in order to drive the enemy out of the place he occupies.

It is therefore necessary in all circumstances to try to advance towards the point that the leader has given as direction.

One stops only when it is impossible to advance.

4. Only one thing can prevent one from advancing: the enemy's fire when it becomes too violent. To fight is precisely to advance in spite of the enemy's fire.

There are two ways to advance in spite of the enemy.

First way: Use the ground to advance without being seen or being seen as much as possible. This is how we advance by leaps and bounds, in open line or a few men at a time, so that the enemy can't just shoot. Usually this means is not enough.

Second way: Shoot the enemy yourself and kill men to scare him into hiding. Then he will not shoot anymore or will shoot badly.

5. You shoot to be able to advance. Fire should only be opened when it is impossible to advance without firing.

Shooting only allows you to advance if the bullets reach the enemy, otherwise it is useless. To shoot too far or without aiming or without seeing the enemy is to waste time and cartridges.

6. How can one advance and shoot at the same time? You aim in groups (sections or half-sections). Some advance while the others shoot.

When you see a neighboring group get up to advance, you must fire violently at the enemy to prevent him from firing at your comrades who are advancing. When you advance yourself, you must always choose your path in such a way as not to prevent the neighboring groups from firing by putting yourself in front of them.

7. In summary, the constant preoccupation of the combatant must be to advance towards the point to be reached and, if at the moment one cannot advance oneself, to help others to advance by shooting at the enemy.

B – Engagement (advance guard)

1. A troop on the move in the vicinity of the enemy always marches towards a well-determined point on the ground, indicated by the leader. It must, in all circumstances and whatever happens, try to reach this point. Usually it is divided into groups (sections or half-sections), each group led by its leader.

2. When the enemy is encountered, one continues to advance, without losing time but using the terrain to hide, towards the point to be reached. If stopped by fire, one attacks.

3. The group that has been forced to stop opens fire to force the enemy to hide and not to fire or to fire badly.

The other groups immediately move off to the right and left, concealing themselves, and continue to advance in order to outflank the enemy and make them leave by taking them in flank.

Then all groups continue their march towards the point to be reached.

C – Defensive

1. One defends only when one *has been ordered* not to attack or when it is impossible to attack.

(Example: a troop waiting for reinforcements, a Grand Guard.)

2. To defend oneself is to prevent the enemy from advancing.

There is only one way: to kill him and wound many men, by shooting at him, so that he is afraid and does not dare to advance.

3. A shot that is not accurate does not stop the enemy and only serves to lose cartridges.

When you can't see the enemy, or you can't see him well, or he is too far away, you must not shoot.

When you can see him well, at a good distance, you must fire violently.

All the time that one is not firing, one must be completely concealed.

4. Fire is not always sufficient to stop the enemy, there is only one thing that succeeds for sure, when one has the heart: it is the attack.

If the enemy advances in spite of the fire, we wait for him at a short distance and when he thinks he is victorious, we throw ourselves on him with the bayonet.

On these bases (completed for other parts of the instruction, such as the service in the field), each officer will be able to compose for the use of his officers and his men a kind of small very short catechism containing only principles expressed in the form of positive and practical precepts while avoiding any discussion and any doubtful expression.

The combat exercises will always be linked to some of these principles and care will be taken to show how the solution adopted is consistent with the precept.

VI – Organization of Instruction – Time Use

There is no time to waste and our training must be intensive while avoiding an overwork which would put off the young soldier. The organization of training is therefore a crucial issue. It is in this area that the captain's initiative will be exercised above all.

Three things are to be considered:

a) Education;

b) Theoretical instruction;

c) Practical training.

A – Education

The question is dealt with in a great number of recent publications; it cannot be given too much importance. We will limit ourselves here to a few remarks.

The question of education is not new. From time immemorial, it has preoccupied the officer conscious of his duties. In the long term service, the education of the man was done naturally by the obliged habituation to certain rules of life and by the daily frequentation of his leaders and his comrades. Short-term service makes the influence of the environment much less profound and forces us to seek artificial means to replace it to a certain extent, and this is what makes some people believe that the education of the soldier dates from today.

We must seek and use these artificial means, but by choosing them and without having too many illusions about their effectiveness.

We are given men to make soldiers of them, as far as possible. Only one thing has a certain educational virtue, and that is the influence of the environment. The officer must therefore strive above all to make this influence moral and to increase its intensity.

Of all the means of education, the surest is the "example." A moral teaching has a practical effect on a man only in so far as that man esteems the teacher. It is therefore necessary that the soldier first esteems his leader and, in this case, every word germinates, every advice bears fruit. Otherwise, no moralizing action is possible. For the officer, to be esteemed is the first duty and the only serious means of education, he must know this. The action of the non-commissioned officers in the same direction will be felt only on the same condition. This being said, we can distinguish two modes of action:

The frequentation of the soldier, the daily conversation, the opinions, the observations of the current life;

The lecture or moral theory.

The first is by far the most important.

To frequent the soldier, to speak to him often, to show interest in him is the only way to acquire influence over him. To direct the minds of his soldiers toward the great questions of morality, the surest thing, moreover, is not to speak about them by profession but to seize every opportunity to show, in one's words and in one's attitude, the esteem one has for the military virtues.

Apart from the usual conversations, it is advisable that the captain speaks to his company once a week. In addition to practical advice and observations, he should always mix in some notions of military duty.

The conference has its value, although it is useless to abuse it. A very good practice is to have it given by a non-commissioned officer, or even by an educated young soldier who is guided in his preparation.

From the point of view of the subjects to be treated, we will note:

That we must aim at making soldiers and, therefore, seek preferably questions of a nature to develop the military spirit;

That it is extremely difficult and useless to deal directly with the great moral questions in their abstract form.

That it is extremely difficult and useless to deal directly with the great moral questions in their abstract form. Documentary accounts, with some remarks intended to bring out the "moral," have much more practical significance. The idea of the Fatherland, for example, and the need to defend it will be suggested not by definitions and empty phrases, but by showing what love of the Fatherland has produced (acts of courage and devotion, feats of arms, great men), and by bringing out the misfortunes of the vanquished (anecdotal accounts of the invasions, the situation of the annexed, etc.).

B – Theoretical training

The so-called theoretical instruction of the soldier is composed of notions and rules, both essentially practical.

Traditionally, this instruction is given in the form of "theories in the rooms," which constitute one of the rites of life of the young soldier. A considerable amount of time is wasted without profit. The theory in the rooms as we know it must disappear almost completely, at least at the beginning of the training.

All the current notions and the rules of daily application which constitute the necessary baggage of the soldier must be taught by the lower ranks, under their responsibility, not in compulsory and supervised sessions of limited duration and on a prescribed subject, but during the free time which, each day, will be left at their disposal for this purpose. The sergeant is in charge of directing this instruction. The captain determines the subjects to be seen and indicates in as precise a manner as possible what the young soldiers are to learn each week; he checks and has the results checked by the officers or the adjutant.

It is important to ensure that the officers do not reintroduce theory in its old form for their own benefit. The teaching must be proportionate to the ability of each individual.

As soon as he knows what he is to be taught, the man has nothing more to do with the theory of the day. The latecomers, on the other hand, will be kept longer, and will be given repetitions by some more advanced comrade. Mutual teaching is to be used to a large extent.

The advantages of this method are multiple: The officer is more interested in an instruction which he directs as he sees fit and for which he is responsible. His time is better spent since he can get rid of the most intelligent ones very quickly. The man, on his side, will learn more quickly, since he works "to the task." This change in morals is rather difficult to obtain, because of the lack of habit of our executives to have a certain initiative.

We will teach all that concerns the internal service, the maintenance of the effects and weapons, the clothing, the ranks, the external marks of respect, the first rules of the service of the places, etc.

Except for the few rules that are taught directly by the officers, the service of the squares will be learned practically in special exercises.

The few indispensable notions on the weapon and on shooting are part of the daily training session of the shooter which will be discussed later.

No theory on field service will be taught in the barracks at the beginning of the training.

Apart from these quite elementary notions and rules learned by applying them, certain subjects must be the subject of prepared "theories." These theories are made by the officers or by non-commissioned officers, on the order of the captain or even by intelligent men with special knowledge.

In this category of prepared theories, or small lectures, fall all those which touch on moral education and tactical instruction. In addition, it should deal with:

Those parts of the training which are somewhat outside the field of current practice (for example: duties of the soldier outside, hygiene, military code, duties of reservists, etc.);

Some questions of a nature to broaden the soldier's military knowledge (on shooting, for example, or field service);

From time to time, a few subjects of general interest that may be of interest to the men and useful to them (agriculture, mutuality, alcoholism, etc.).

N.B. – We speak to be understood. But it would be as unreasonable to keep to the level of a few illiterates as to speak only for an elite. Except for technical subjects requiring special knowledge, the average of our men can reach higher than is sometimes thought, provided that the ideas are clearly presented.

C. - Practical training

The practical training is, for the troop, especially of the dressage. It is a question of bringing the man (individual training) or the troop (collective training) to execute correctly, without fatigue and, so to speak, mechanically – that is to say with the minimum of attention – a small number of movements and evolutions. One must therefore obtain both physical training and habits.

In spite of its interest, we will not deal here with the question of training, which requires a separate study.

From what has been said above about individual and group training, it is clear that our goal in organizing practical training will be twofold:

1. To arrive very quickly at the execution of useful movements, so as to be able to repeat them daily for a long time;

2. To vary as much as possible the occupations of the man to

avoid disgust and overwork. There is another reason of great practical value, to begin as soon as possible and to push during the first period the exercises of collective easing and the service in field. Generally speaking, in our French garrisons, it is only during the late autumn and part of the winter that one can maneuver in the countryside. One must not lose a day to take advantage of this precious benefit.

All the branches of the young soldier's instruction (gymnastics and flexibility, training of the man, training of the gunner, training of the group, service in the field) will therefore be started from the beginning and continued in parallel.

D – Schedule

Each day of instruction between reveille and the evening meal shall include during the first period of instruction:

A rest of at least one hour, including the time for the morning meal;

A certain amount of time during which the men are at the disposal of the company's officers for interior instruction–time that varies according to the use of the day and is quite long during the first weeks.

The rest of the day is devoted to training proper, which will include a daily session of gymnastics and flexibility and another for training the shooter. From the second week onwards, there will also be a daily group training session.

Practically every afternoon of good weather (except for one afternoon per week for cleaning and rest and another, on Saturday, for cleanliness, reviews and training checks) will be used for outdoor exercises in the countryside.

These varied exercises must be carefully organized and directed, and it is here that the intelligence and ability of the platoon officers will be displayed.

They may include "close range" on the roads, group instruction, field service, including the use of terrain and parts of the gunner's training, such as target searches, distance assessment, etc.

These long outdoor sessions and the free training of the soldier through the fields constitute both the best of all training and an excellent training process.

As of December 1st, a night session and a road march will be added each week, almost always interspersed with an exercise in varied terrain.

For all the exercises, the bag will be taken empty at first and then little by little weighed down, following a slow progression.

Every Sunday, the captain will give to the battalion commander, not the forecasts for the training of the week that is beginning – forecasts that are always vague and put in default by circumstances – but the report of the training actually given in the week that is ending. This report will take the following form.

Instruction during the past week from _____ to _____

I - Internal Instruction and Theories

A. By the staff during free hours.   . . . .
. . . .
. . . .
. . . .
B. By the officers: Soldiers. . . . .
. . . .
Cadres. . . . .
. . . .
C. Theory or supervised lectures   . . . .
   (selected officers or men)   . . . .
. . . .
. . . .

II – Military training and maneuvers

A. Relaxation and gymnastics.   . . . .
. . . .
. . . .
. . . .
B. Shooting.   . . . .
. . . .
. . . .
C. Maneuver: Individual instruction . . . .
. . . .
   Group training.   . . . .
. . . .
   Field service.   . . . .
. . . .

III - Former soldiers

. . . .
. . . .
. . . .

Booklet 2– Training of the Gunner

Contents

Fencer Training

To see how incomplete the training of the fencer for combat is usually, one would be tempted to think that it is an accessory. It is, on the contrary, of all the parts of the training, the one that requires the most care and must absorb the most time. The little importance that is often given to it in our time schedule explains how we can sometimes see captains embarrassed to "occupy" their men and would be of a nature to strengthen this opinion, too widespread in the public, that it takes little time to train a soldier.

It is important to react. The principles that will guide us in this task are the following:

There is no collective shooting obeying special laws. In combat, there are men firing simultaneously, each of them intending to reach for his own account the goal he aims at.

Sometimes, the man can be guided in the choice of the rise, the objective, etc... This is the guided shot. *More often, in the offensive fight he will be left to himself.*

The instruction of the shooting therefore consists almost entirely in the individual instruction. This instruction, to be usable in combat, must be mainly training.

The rules of fire control must be as simple as possible and the man must be accustomed to do without the direction of the leader if necessary.

The regulation of August 31, 1905 ensures the instructor a very broad initiative. It is only a question here of specifying in which direction we can usefully exercise this initiative.

I – Individual Training

Even more so in shooting than in any other part of training, it is important to remember that individual training is not intended to standardize men and cast them in the same mold, but to obtain from each man the maximum useful output.

We seek, therefore, to have each man do the best he can, without attaching any importance to his doing the same as others.

§1 – Technical Training

It is a question of teaching a man to shoot well; it is therefore mainly training. There is only one method: to arrive quickly at useful movements and to repeat them as often as possible.

The great difficulty is to bring the young soldier to repeat these movements "usefully," that is to say not to be satisfied with a simple simulacrum. The instructor concludes that he must :

Make the men understand the reason for each movement;

Spend all his time giving "private lessons" by training the men successively;

Avoid disgust by making the sessions frequent but short and relatively varied;

Concentrate his efforts on the useful use of the ammunition allocated, because to learn to shoot well, the best way is still to practice shooting.

1. Preparatory exercises

The exercises of pointing on the bridge must be proportionate to the needs of each man. Some will have to be practiced for a long time, while others will be able to point correctly very quickly.

As soon as one has noticed that a man points regularly, it is useless to make him waste his time looking at the clumsy ones.

Aiming exercises are very important. One should not do aiming exercises without aiming, because it is only by aiming that the man will see if his aiming is good. It is therefore necessary to arrive as quickly as possible at the useful movement: "Aim at a point in an indicated position." This exercise will be repeated every day, as often as possible in the countryside, not only in the regulation positions but using the accidents of the terrain and insisting on the usual positions of combat shooting (lying or crouching behind obstacles of little height: ridges, earthen levees, the reverse side of ditches, etc.).

The education of the eye is a capital point, it is important to start it from the beginning. The points to be aimed at, placed at a short distance and easy to distinguish in the first sessions, will be quickly moved away to arrive at the usual distances of combat: 400-800 meters. We will often use low silhouettes whose color can be varied and, above all, we will take advantage of all the outings to aim at visible objects in the countryside, especially at men in different positions.

To combat the natural tendency to shoot too high, it is recommended to choose targets that are low to the ground and to always aim at the foot of the target. The weapon in the "cheek" movement should come to the shoulder, the barrel slightly tilted toward the ground, and the shooter should aim by raising the end of the barrel.

The physical training of the shooter consists almost solely of the very frequent repetition of the complete act of the shooter: "Load, aim and shoot in all positions." Article 20 of the rules defines this perfectly.

Inconvenient positions (e.g., supply, load, and fire lying down behind a low shelter) will be emphasized, and it will be well to impose upon the men fairly long sessions of these exercises, requiring them to load, aim, and fire without interruption. The fatigue produced at the end of only a few minutes of this relaxation is enough to show its usefulness. It can be prolonged for ten minutes, a quarter of an hour, or half an hour, explaining to the shooters beforehand that they will have to fight in this way sometimes for a very long time.

2. Shooting exercises

Live firing is the only complete preparation exercise for combat firing; it is also the most useful. In practice, one is limited by the cartridge allocations; one must at least put all one's care into using them judiciously.

The shooting is only profitable under the following conditions: To be of difficulty proportionate to the shooter's skill. A shot that is too difficult, where he can only succeed by chance, only serves to disgust him;

To be organized in such a way that the results can be easily and surely observed;

Be organized in such a way that the results can be easily and surely observed; Include a sanction, at least moral, by the interest that the officers of the company take in it and the encouragements given to the good shooters.

It is completely useless to try to lead all the men in the same way. The shooting at short range will be started very early for some of them, while others will have to be led in front of the target only after a longer preparation. It will be necessary, therefore, to know and watch the present value of each shooter, first in the section and then in the company, if successful training is to be made.

Live shots at close range are the best beginning instruction when circumstances permit them to be made at leisure. One can insist on these shots and obtain excellent results, provided that one only asks the shooter to shoot at the goal when his groupings are regularly good. It is advisable to gradually increase the difficulty by changing the color and size of the visuals.

They should be replaced, when necessary, by reduced shots which are certainly less advantageous, but which can be more numerous.

In *instructional shooting*, the aim is to get the shooter to apply, at practical distances, what he knows. If he is really confirmed in shooting at reduced distances, it is above all a matter of the eye. We will therefore tend towards the extreme ranges (300-400 meters), but not losing sight of the fact that the shooter must be able to see the result of almost all his shots. If he loses too many of his bullets, we bring him back to the distances where he can usefully shoot.

The soldier can only take advantage of the *application shots* when he knows how to use his rifle. We will thus admit him to these shootings only when, until 400 meters, he will regularly put 50% of his bullets in the circle of diameter equal to the two-hundredth of the distance.

It is especially in the organization of these shots that it is necessary to remember that a too difficult shot, in which the man can hope for success only by chance, is useless. Our application shots will therefore be, at the beginning, rather easy and in any case proportionate to the strength of our shooters. It is not necessary that each soldier has done in his year the same shots as his comrades. The important thing is that he benefits from the ones he executes, because, despite the title of "application shooting," it is in reality special training shooting.

The importance of the practice shooting is not in doubt; it is the necessary transition between the range and the combat.

The man must learn to shoot "under conditions approaching those of war," that is to say:

a) In practical positions, using natural or artificial accidents to evade and support his weapon. This requires an arrangement, always easy, of the shooting range;

b) On targets of different shape and color, approaching the probable targets of war. It is very useful, in particular, to imagine objectives that are wider than they are high and always close to the ground; for example, heads or busts forming a band at the lower part of a large target, in preference to separate silhouettes, so as to be able to see the shots close to the target. The target should then be covered with grey or yellowish paper that is close to the color of the ground;

c) In certain conditions of dress and fatigue: full field dress, after a walk or a violent exercise or after a prolonged session of shooting with false cartridges;

d) By making the corrections necessary by the use of the combat elevation, by the wind or by the movement of the target.

It would certainly be desirable to always use the combat elevator at short distances. In practice, because of the small number of cartridges to be burned and to encourage the man by making him obtain better results, one will be led sometimes, in the difficult shots, to take the exact rise;

e) Finally, taking into account the duration. It is very important to accustom the man to shoot quickly. But this requires a special education and some precautions.

One should be careful not to make the time intervene for the first time in a difficult shot. It is advisable, on the contrary, to choose a very easy shot in which the results will surely be noticed, for example a shot at reduced distance. Everyone will use the tricks they deem appropriate. One can advise shooting on command as it is done for pistol shooting, by first giving ample time to aim and only accelerating little by little.

When organizing the practice shots, the following points should be taken into account:

Only gradually increase the difficulty;

Give the student the very important notion that one shoots quickly at an easy goal and more slowly at a difficult one. In order to be understood, one can use eclipse goals of different sizes, the smaller ones remaining visible for a longer period of time;

Do not be satisfied with always noting the result obtained in a given time, but also the time necessary to obtain a determined result: as, for example, to shoot down two or three falling silhouettes. This is undoubtedly the best way to give the notion of "shooting efficiency."

The organization of real shooting appropriate to the needs of training presents serious difficulties because of the insufficiency of our shooting ranges. The biggest obstacle does not come from their restricted dimensions or the bad equipment; one can organize on almost all of them a series of instructional and application shootings which are more or less sufficient. What makes, in many garrisons, the training so difficult to conduct seriously, is the little time given to each unit for the execution of its shots.

It is essential to proportion the difficulty of the shooting to the means of the man; it is the basis of any reasonable individual training.

This requires that several different shots be organized during each session given to the company. The captain will often find it impossible to do this. There is only one way to alleviate this serious inconvenience, and that is to make an agreement between companies.

As soon as the instructional shootings are sufficiently advanced for it to be possible to make a serious classification of the shooters, the captains of the same battalion can meet at the end of the week and agree on the organization, for the following week, of two or three shootings of different difficulty between which they will distribute the shooters according to their needs.

This attack on the complete autonomy of the companies is not without disadvantages, but it will often be impossible to act otherwise. In addition, the obligation for the captains to frequently pool, under the direction of the battalion commander, their ideas on the organization of fire, presents some advantages.

§2 – Tactical Instruction

The wording of the rules (§32 and following) may give rise to a misunderstanding that must be avoided. One should not confuse the shooting of the isolated man with individual shooting.

The man may be guided in some cases by the indication of the elevation, the objective, the moment when he must open fire, etc. In this case, the shot is said to be "individual." In these cases, the shooting is said to be "guided." In other cases, very frequent in combat, he will have, even in a group, to do without these indications and act by himself. The tactical instruction of the shooter is intended to teach him what he must know to use his weapon usefully whenever the shooting is not conducted.

It is a very important and too neglected part of our preparation for combat; it requires a lot of time. This instruction will necessarily be given to several men at once. It must be started from the beginning with that of the field service and continued throughout the year. Moreover, live-fire experience is necessary to complete it.

What we want to teach the men can be summed up in two questions:

When to shoot?

How to shoot?

1. When to shoot ?

A man must shoot in all circumstances with the intention of hitting. If there is not enough probability to hit, he does not shoot. It is thus a question of first giving the young soldier the notion of the "probability of hitting," then of putting him in a position to appreciate practically this probability.

The notion of the "probability of hitting" according to the apparent size of the target and its visibility will come out especially from the real shooting. During the shooting, one should insist on this point of view, talk to the men about this subject, show them groupings at different distances. They will be made to realize that distance is not the only element; the lighting, the color, the movement of the target modify a lot the chances of reaching it (silhouettes of different colors, partly hidden, mobile..., the same ones against the light, at dusk, etc.).

Now that you have this notion, how do you apply it? First, one must learn to "see" and then to judge whether or not to shoot, taking into account the general case of a man in combat.

The particular case of the isolated man is examined separately.

The exercises to obtain these results are :

Searching for objectives; aiming at all kinds of goals;

Appreciation by each man if he has a chance to reach.

The appreciation of distances is part of these exercises. It must be admitted that the man does not appreciate to choose his rise. With rare exceptions that must be neglected, when the shot is not conducted, the soldier always uses the combat elevation. If he looks for the distance to the target, it is to know if he should shoot and to make some elementary corrections (shoot a little lower, a little to the right or to the left). Therefore, man only needs to appreciate with a very large approximation the usual distances of combat and we should only ask him what is necessary. By very frequent exercises organized with goals and on varied grounds, we can hope that the soldier will get "in the eye" a very small number of distances, for example: 250, 500, 800 meters. These distances will serve as a guide and when presented with an objective, he will not try to indicate the distance, but only to say whether he is closer or further than one of the standard distances.

In the goal-seeking exercises through the countryside, the goal being discovered, the men, including those who cannot see for some cause, will be questioned in a form similar to the following:

Q. Do you shoot?   A. I don't shoot.

Q. Why?   A. I can't see or I can't see well enough.
It's too far away (beyond 800 meters).
They are too few for the distance (four or five men over 500 meters).
They move too fast, etc.

Q. Do you shoot?   A. I shoot.

Q. Why?   A. Sufficient group between 500 and 800 meters.
Target closer than 500 meters, etc.

These exercises should be varied often, but it is very useful to repeat the same one several times in different weather and at different times (rain, fog, snow, dusk, etc.). We will insist on the usual distances of combat (500-800 meters); we usually work on too small distances.

The case of isolated men, or in very small groups (double sentry, patrol) will be treated separately, showing that the fact of shooting or not shooting is always subordinated to tactical circumstances, whatever the probability of hitting.

Examples: One shoots, even without any chance of hitting, when it is necessary to give the alarm and when one has no other way to warn. You don't shoot, even if you are sure to hit, when you want to hide your presence (patrols, ambushes).

This is proper service in the field.

2. How to shoot ?

We will always let the man choose his position. While checking it, insist on the necessity to see well and not to be seen. If one does not see or if one sees badly, one must move. To learn the defilement, a good procedure is to have the men work in two opposing groups.

We shoot to hit. It is the ease of reaching the goal that regulates the speed. The more difficult the shot, the more carefully it should be aimed.

If the goal disappears, you stop shooting.

This principle is the only basis of fire discipline for a troop left to its own devices. It is not enough to make it understood, it must, by long training, be transformed into a habit so that in combat something remains of it.

The man always uses - unless otherwise ordered - the combat rise. But he must, according to the distance, the atmospheric circumstances or the particularities of the weapon, make some elementary corrections.

In the tactical training exercises of the shooter, after having asked him: "Are you shooting? Why are you shooting?" he will be asked to indicate the point he is aiming at, then his position and the speed of his shooting will be checked, requiring him to stop shooting immediately as soon as the objective disappears.

3. Combat shooting

The individual shots of combat, such as one can organize them usually, enter partly in the shots of application defined above, partly in the first shots of the group of which it is question below.

To make an isolated man choose his elevator is not to be recommended; on the contrary, it is very useful to multiply the shots with the combat elevator at all distances.

The "probability of hitting" can be emphasized by showing targets of varying size and visibility; the man deciding whether or not to shoot.

Target changes would be very useful at the usual combat distances, but they can rarely be usefully organized on our ranges and even in training camps.

II – Group instruction

The regulation of August 21, 1905 limits its action, as regards the collective instruction, to the group; i.e. to a small number of men obeying without intermediary to the same chief

The strength of the combat group is limited by experience. We have accepted as typical the peacetime section (wartime half-section), which is, practically, twenty or twenty-five men. It can be and often will be less strong. For training, the group formed at the beginning of a very small number of men is gradually brought to the strength of the peacetime section.

The part of the training which consists in making the men physically carry out a command – such as to take a certain rise or to open fire when ordered to do so – is not, strictly speaking, shooting instruction, since the technical part is the concern of the cadres only; this is discussed later. For the troop, it is a relaxation similar to the others.

The really important and difficult part of the group training is all negative. It is a question of obtaining that the men do not lose, when they shoot together, the habits acquired in the individual shooting. This means that, driven or not driven, each of them must, under all circumstances, shoot with the firm intention of reaching for his own account the goal he aims at. The only new positive notion to be acquired in group shooting is that of fire distribution.

The two main rules to be taught practically can be formulated as follows:

The value of group shooting depends absolutely on the value of each man's shooting. One must therefore always shoot for one's own account with the same care as if one were alone;

When the target is large, which is the general case in combat, everyone must shoot at the part of the target that is in front of him, unless he cannot see it or is ordered otherwise.

To obtain this result, the instruction of the man in the group must remain as long as possible "individual." Therefore, no clear distinction will be made in outdoor exercises between the tactical training of the gunner and that of the group. The soldiers will be trained as indicated above (tactical training of the shooter) in groups initially small enough so that each of them can be easily monitored and questioned.

The group will then be increased to the strength of the section, without any change in the manner of questioning, so as to give that impression that – regardless of the strength – the man must shoot for his own account with the same attention. These exercises of individual shooting "in group" will be pushed to 600 to 800 meters, without the chief intervening other than as an instructor, by checking and correcting the way of acting of the shooters.

Only then, and at greater distances, will the exercises of "controlled shooting" begin. Only the distance and not the number of shooters in the group determines whether the shooting should be conducted or free.

In these conducted fire sessions one should carefully avoid turning the exercise into a "weapons drill" – as is too often seen – by having numerous commands of "such and such a rise, such and such a target, commence fire, cease fire....." hurriedly executed. This has no real significance. The instructor, after indicating the target and distance, will have the men open fire, then let them settle down and continue firing while he individually interviews as many as possible; checking the position, the elevation, the part of the target aimed at, the speed of fire.

It is necessary that the men have the impression that the conducted shooting differs from the non-conducted shooting only by this fact: the distance being greater, it is the leader of the group who decides whether to shoot or not, who recognizes and designates the objective and who indicates to each shooter, to facilitate his task, the elevation to be used.

Outdoor training exercises must be carefully prepared. It takes time, care and ingenuity to ensure that the movements of the target groups permit useful observations and that distances are well marked. Companies should be encouraged to assist each other in this task, and there is no disadvantage in having several companies use the same exercise successively.

To take into account the consistent lessons of recent wars,

showing the discovery of the enemy as one of the main difficulties of the attack, special emphasis should be placed on the search for and change of objectives, operating frequently at medium distances, 800 to 1,500 meters, and sometimes at long distances.

§1 – Group Shooting

Our firing will be proportionate to the strength of the shooters and organized in such a way that the results obtained are known to all and can be compared. The groups will be formed as much as possible of constituted fractions (section, half-section, squad, etc.) commanded by their usual instructors.

The men will be agglomerated only gradually, and the line of two men will be fired first, then four or five men, etc.

In the first shots, it is advantageous to have as many particular targets as there are men, so as to bring out in the total result the part taken by each shooter.

The man will be free to choose his position and, within a fixed limit, his location. As soon as there is no longer one target per man, he will also have to choose his target and the distribution of the shot will be taken into account. As often as possible, the time used to obtain the result will also be taken into account. The tricks necessary to make these elements enter the appreciation of the shooting are easy to imagine.

In all the non-conducted shootings the combat rise will be compulsory.

It will often be difficult to organize group shooting for several reasons:

Limitation of the number of cartridges to be burned;

Insufficient shooting ranges;

Lack of time. The unit having the range only for a very limited time will not be able to train its shooters according to their skills.

These disadvantages can be mitigated. A large part of the cartridges spent in the past in "war shooting" will be "employed in group shooting which, well organized, constitutes the best preparation for combat shooting.

Among these shots, the most useful are those of the small group, with no other tactical hypothesis than that of advancing on the enemy by killing him. The necessary equipment can be organized at a fairly low cost; it is necessary in this order of ideas to be ingenious.

Finally, the very serious difficulty of organizing different shots according to the strength of the shooters has already been examined. The companies of the same battalion will have to agree among themselves.

As an example, let us point out the following organization of a group shooting:

The objective is formed by several separate groups of falling silhouettes more or less hidden and difficult to see, on a sufficient front.

The terrain, from the extreme distance where we want to start shooting, is divided into a number of irregular slices from 50 to 100 meters deep. The limits are marked by flags.

The group making an approach march in the desired direction is stopped – at the moment chosen by the director of the exercise – by the supposed shooting of the enemy. From that moment on, the group leader has his freedom, under the condition that he cannot pass from one zone to the next until he has shot one or more silhouettes of each of the groups in the line of objectives.

It is easy to vary and insist on time, ammunition consumed, ground gained, etc. It is also possible to set a limit at which fire will no longer be conducted.

§2 – Cadre Training

In cadre training, one must consider:
Preparation for their duties as fire instructors;
Preparation for their role in the conduct of fire.

Having admitted that it is the value of each individual shooter that makes the effectiveness of the shooting, we will conclude without hesitation that the preparation for the functions of instructor is the most important. The foregoing considerations obviate the need for further discussion.

The preparation for the conduct of fire itself consists of two parts:
Tactical instruction, intended to guide the decision of the

group leader;

Practical methods to be used to conduct the fire and to make the instruction of the group accordingly.

The tactical instruction of the cadres is, in short, very similar to that of the shooters and is given in similar exercises, with the only difference that the distances will be greater. It is always a question of discovering objectives and estimating the probability of reaching them.

In the decision (Should we shoot? How to shoot?) will enter, it is true, more elements. The appreciation or measurement of distances and the choice of the rise take, because of the distance, a preponderant place in the probability to reach. In addition, the tactical situation determining the result to be obtained will always come into play.

In the theoretical instruction of the executives, it is advisable to avoid as much as possible the considerations of "sheaves" and "cores," or at least to indicate that these words are simply images not answering any reality. It is possible and preferable to say simply: If one makes moderately educated men shoot on a polygon, at such a distance, with the exact rise, each of them will have a certain chance to reach a goal of given height. At the same distance, with such and such an error in the rise, the chance is reduced to half; with such and such an error, to a tenth, etc. As the probability of hitting, for a group, is only the sum of the individual probabilities of the shooters who compose it, it is easy to estimate, for a given distance, from which error of rise the shot would have no more value.

It remains for us to examine the role of the group leader in collective shooting exercises.

We have accepted the following principles:

The leader in combat will exercise his action on the fire of his men all the longer that this action will be simpler and reduced to the necessary things.

It is really not a matter of "leading fire" but of leading and directing men who fire. It is more important to put one's men in good material and moral conditions to fire than to give "right" commands.

It will often happen that, for shooting, the soldier in combat will be reduced to his own means.

Therefore, in the group exercises for combat shooting, one should : Remove everything that is not necessary; insist on the really useful points; accustom the man to act by himself. In particular :

The position to be taken will not be indicated. The soldier must choose for himself the one that allows him to escape and to shoot at ease. Nothing is more implausible and useless than to command "Lie down," at every bound.

When the enemy on whom one is firing disappears, one should not command: "Cease fire"; but demand that the men stop firing on their own.

The rise will only be indicated when it differs from the combat rise. Moreover, in outdoor exercises, one should never order a raise lower than the combat raise.

One will get into the habit of always ceasing to conduct fire at small distances (400, 600 meters).

It is advisable to insist, on the contrary, on the "recognition" of the objective. To make the fighters see the target on which they must shoot is a difficult and very important point. One should also watch the distribution of the shot, which is too often neglected.

There remains the question of *fire discipline.*

It is necessary to know that a command will never be enough to prevent a man from firing when he receives bullets and sees or thinks he sees the one who is sending them. He must therefore be helped to obey by putting him in such a situation that he cannot shoot, or at least by keeping him in a formation where he is not accustomed to shoot.

Fire discipline is summed up in two rules:

The un-driven man fires only when he can usefully do so (individual discipline);

A man who is led shoots only on the order of his leader (collective discipline).

We have already indicated the habits that promote individual discipline:

Never shoot when you can't see yourself. Always shoot with the will to reach, that is to say, all the more calmly when the objective is more difficult.

To facilitate collective discipline, we will adopt the following habits in our exercises:

Require that at each stop, the man disappear completely behind his cover and take up his firing position only on the order of the leader, at the moment of opening fire. If there is no cover and one is within firing distance, open fire immediately.

To stop the fire, make the man disappear behind his shelter. If there is no cover – to cease fire, move forward or at least change places.

In approaching marches or in the march of supports behind the line of fire: never deploy an advance in skirmishers other than for a very short time, as a process of marching. At each stop, keep your group together and hidden so that the men cannot see ahead.

The fire with counted cartridges can be useful provided that the men are hidden. In this case, a fire limited to a very small number of cartridges (1 to 3) is ordered, which are held in the hand or placed on the ground in advance. As soon as these cartridges are fired, the man returns to his shelter.

Act in the same way for the rapid fires "with eclipse"; the men get up in their trench or behind their shelter the time necessary to make the ordered shooting. In combat exercises it is necessary to limit the number of blank cartridges for each shot; but it will be required that the man continues to shoot without blank cartridges as long as the fire must not cease.

Remarks. – Usually, our combat training is very neglected with regard to shooting, whereas it is on the contrary the part which should absorb the most time.

As soon as it is no longer a question of actual drill, the combat exercises in the company will be mainly fire exercises. One will not try to carry out the whole combat; two or three jumps can be enough for an exercise. However, the enemy's image will be carefully prepared in advance, and may vary, be reinforced, advance or retreat, disappear, etc. The stops will be very long in order to watch and question a large number of men. The others will find the opportunity to do long periods of shooting with false cartridges.

Thus limited, these exercises will allow the use of restricted open spaces in the countryside separated from the enemy's location by cultivated or impassable land.

We will insist on the usual distances of combat (800, 500 meters).

Booklet 3 – Easing of the Section and the Company in dispersed order

Combat Training of the Section and the Company

The purpose of training troops for combat is to form a strong and flexible tool of war, safe and easy to handle.

The purpose of training officers is to teach them to handle this tool and to get the most out of it.

As far as the conduct of combat is concerned, the training of officers can and must be limited to a few principles, based on experience, intended to enlighten their decisions and regulate their initiative.

The training of the troops, on the other hand, can only be obtained by the frequent repetition of the same movements, and must be based on more precise regulations. Among the possible procedures of combat, of route, of shooting, etc., it is thus necessary to make a choice, to translate these procedures into rules and to transform these rules into habits by a repeated application. The set of procedures thus chosen and taught constitutes the detailed tactics of the weapon. The role of the rules is to set the main lines.

Collective flexibility is a significant part of training; its importance has increased considerably as a result of the new requirements of combat.

Our regulations are not very explicit on this subject, as far as the dispersed order is concerned; moreover, they leave a very broad initiative to the instructors. It is only a question here of choosing, among the movements ordered or authorized by the regulations, those which are likely to make the lower units flexible and suitable for combat, in order to insist on them in our instruction and to give them the "habit" to the troops.

The following indications concern :

1. The easing of the section (combat group). We will use the word "section" here, observing that everything that follows applies to any group of men obeying the same leader without intermediary.

The size of the peacetime section or the wartime half-section (20-25 men) seems to be the maximum for an easily manageable combat group.

2. The easing of the company (several sections obeying the same leader).

I – Easing up the section

Flexibility exercises should, by frequent repetition, become as familiar to the men as shooting or handling weapons. They include only elementary movements that can be performed without any tactical assumptions. This training of the group for combat must become one of the principal parts of our training.

§1 – Deployments

With the section in any formation, deploy it in any direction

Insist on direct skirmisher deployment of the column in fours or pairs.

Remarks. – The transition from a marching or mustering formation to a thin line formation is the basis of all training of troops for combat. One must, by very frequent exercises, manage to get the men to deploy quickly, without disorder and facing the indicated point.

Deployments without any indication of objective or

perpendicular to the direction of march – are to be omitted as a matter of course – to deploy always "facing something."

Deployments will alternate with assembling in one or two ranks, either on foot or to continue the march. One always assembles behind the instructor who has himself facing the point he indicates as direction.

The deployment in a row without intervals (which is too often considered normal deployment) should not be the sole or even the main object of this training. The full line thus obtained is too tight to walk, use the ground and shoot at ease.

Men must be trained, by daily practice, to deploy and walk in a more open line.

Each deployment at open intervals would require, to become quick and regular, special relaxation.

We will limit ourselves practically to a small number of intervals which we will make familiar to the men by frequent repetition.

We will choose two of them:

The two-step deployment which is very suitable for a dense line; it will be our usual deployment.

The five-step deployment which, without being very difficult to obtain, already constitutes a flexible line, not very vulnerable and not easily visible at great distances.

N.B. – As soon as the section is in skirmishers, the usual position is the "conched" position.

§2 – Walks

Walking exercises over fairly large areas, especially in a two-step and five-step extended line (do them, when possible, on difficult terrain or in the woods; at each stop, have the student lie down).

Remarks. – Do not lose an opportunity to make everyone apply the major principle (too often lost sight of) of our current rules. Everyone must know the direction of travel, face it, and walk straight on; this is the main thing. The duty of every honest man to walk at about the same height as his neighbors and to try to keep his interval on the side of the guide comes only afterwards.

§3 - Change of Direction

With the section deployed, face it in any direction immediately.
This movement will usually be followed by the immediate
opening of fire.
    Remarks. – Get the movement done very quickly and get the
men to face the point indicated. In a large section, accustom the
pivotal half-section to open fire without waiting for the whole
section to be placed.

§4 – Moving Forward By Successive Jumps

1. Carry forward the deployed section (in combat)

A – Make the entire section jump

With the section lying on its position, as little time as possible
should elapse between the time the men rise and the time they
again lie on the next position.
    No previous movement, no noise on the line should make one
suspect that the section is going to get up.
    Remarks. – The following may be done: The section leader and
the ranks are behind their men, in the same position or at least
completely concealed.
    The section leader warns that they are going to move forward,
gives the indications he can give on the direction, the new position
to be occupied and even, if necessary, on the fire to be opened on
arrival. These instructions were repeated half-heartedly by the
leaders of the half-section and the officers, and the men
communicated them to each other.
    Once this is done, the section leader blows a whistle or orders
"Forward," gets up, goes forward and starts to fire. He gets up and
runs forward, the whole line follows him. Having reached the
position to be occupied, the section leader throws himself to the
ground, everyone imitates him.
    The movements of standing up and digging in must be done
very quickly and without hesitation.

B – With the section deployed, move it to another forward
position in small groups

At training, groups of four or five men will usually be trained by
a selected officer or soldier.

Remarks. – It can be executed as follows:

The section leader indicates to a sure rank the new shelter to
be reached. The officer takes with him three or four men (these
men would be chosen, in reality, among the bravest and most
vigorous), runs there followed by his men and establishes himself
at the point where the right (or the left) of the section should be.

The section leader then sends off his groups of four or five
men in succession, indicating whether they should go to the left or
right of the groups already established. He leaves with the last
group.

The men of each small group should not, during the journey,
huddle together or follow each other in line, but, on the contrary,
fan out to form an open line. It is well to accustom them also not
to group in a pack on arrival, but to occupy the new shelter in such
a way that each one is at ease to fire.

It will be indicated whether the firing is to be resumed by each
small group as soon as it is placed or whether the men are to wait,
completely concealed, until the whole section is assembled.

2. With the section under cover, assemble it behind another
shelter by crossing a dangerous zone (approach march)

A – In small groups

As above. The men gather behind the new shelter.

B – In very open single file, the men following each other at five
or ten paces

This movement is very frequently used in cut country and to use
narrow paths (hedges, ditches...)

To obtain that the men leave at their distance without loss of
time and do not form packs by joining together during the journey.

Get them used to using low shelters and shallow cuts by running or walking leaning forward.

C - Very open line (five steps and sometimes more)

Depending on the front that is available, one starts in groups of varying numbers (squad, half-section), previously deployed before leaving the shelter, at large intervals; each line starts moving as soon as the previous one is buried, if the distance is small (less than 100 meters).

If the distance is greater, the lines can be followed at 100 or 150 meters.

Exercise to be done while running for small distances, without running if the distance is large.

N.B. – 1. Always be concerned with activating the movement. Formations that are too diluted cause such a waste of time that with large numbers they would often become impossible.

2. Never forget to assemble your group whenever possible.

§5 – Occupation of Shooting Positions – Fire

Require that after a march or leap the men always stop behind the ridge or shelter to be occupied, and disappear completely by lying down to blow while the leader, concealed as best he can, observes and gives directions for firing if necessary.

This rule is general.

When the fire is to be started, the firing point, on the order of the section leader, is reached by crawling so as to show oneself as little as possible and only at the moment of firing.

Practice the men to disappear completely on a signal and then resume firing in the same way.

In principle, for shooting, the lines will be opened to two paces, which corresponds to one man per meter. If you want to extend your line, you should do so by forming several separate groups rather than by widening the intervals between the men too much. However, the men should be accustomed to filling a line at more open intervals (five paces).

Exercise of rapid fire. – With the men lying down or kneeling, completely sheltered behind a ridge, a trench, a ditch, etc., have them approach and give the necessary indications for firing. At the signal of the whistle, the men get up, make a short burst as violent as possible (generally standing, repetitive fire), then, at a second whistle, disappear behind their shelter. This procedure must be made familiar to the men. (the rapid fires "with complete eclipses" constitute the weapon of the close defense.

N.B. - This habit given to the men of standing habitually. quite concealed behind the firing position and of occupying that position only on an order from the leader, and then disappearing again, is extremely important. It is perhaps the only practical means of regulating the consumption of ammunition and of obtaining discipline of fire.

General observation

The section or group stretching exercises must always be directed by an officer. Make them less long but very serious; repeat the same one several times in a row until perfect execution.

To make the NCOs and the men understand the usefulness of this instruction. Explain what each one of them can be used for. Finally and above all, take advantage of every opportunity to apply them during maneuvers and combat exercises.

II – Company training

The training of the company in view of the fight aims especially at the instruction of the section leaders. It is not intended, like the easing of the group, to make the men execute correctly certain elementary movements, but rather to make familiar, by a repeated application, certain rules of solidarity.

The company is a group of several sections which the captain uses as he sees fit, with a view to the goal to be reached. In each particular case, the captain's intentions being known, the section leader uses, to fulfill them, the procedures to which he has previously trained his section (relaxation of the group).

Often, in order to march and fight, the company will be divided into groups smaller than the section. It is therefore very useful, in the flexibility exercises, to sometimes practice leading more than four groups.

§1 - Deployments

The company does not normally deploy as a whole at once in skirmishes. The sections deploy, each on its own account, facing the direction prescribed and taking the interval indicated between them.

It may be necessary, however, to act by fire as quickly as possible in a given direction; for example, in case of surprise or cavalry attack. It is therefore necessary to press the movements that allow to obtain this result.

> 1. The company being in a marching formation or in an assembly, form it in line in any direction

The sections being relaxed, everything depends on the presence of mind of the section leaders.

It is unnecessary for all the sections to be on the same line, as long as each of them is established facing the indicated point and that all can fire. For this purpose, it is advisable to always take a certain interval between the sections.

This movement will generally be followed by a rapid fire. Each section will start firing as soon as it is placed.

One can sometimes make immediate deployments with rapid fire starting from formations of assembly, formed beams, broken ranks.

> 2. The company being deployed, face it at any point

Same observations as above. Very often only a part of the company will be established in the new direction.

§2 - Approach Marches

> 1. March the entire company in open formation

A – All sections at once

The formation naturally depends on the circumstances. The sections may march in a single line, in a chessboard, in echelons, etc. Each section being in line or in column (in this case, preferably in column by two), and free moreover to change momentarily its formation according to the needs of the march.

When training and whatever the formation, usually take intervals at least three times the front of the section in two ranks. To march over fairly long distances when the terrain lends itself to it.

Remarks. – Everyone must know the direction. If the point designated by the captain is not far enough away, the section leader chooses one for himself a little to the right or left depending on his place in relation to the base unit, and indicates it to his men.

The intervals and the distances are preserved in the whole of the movement, but one should not seek the rigidity of the formation and leave him always, on the contrary, a certain elasticity.

B – The sections marching in succession

The captain indicates the direction, the intervals, the number of sections that must march at the same time and, if he deems it appropriate, their formation.

At the instruction, the following procedure can be insisted upon.

The sections, generally in columns of two, are placed at intervals as wide as the terrain or the area of march assigned to the company will permit. Only one section marches at a time; as soon as it is bogged down, another rises and makes a leap in the direction indicated, taking care to pass the halted sections very noticeably. The leaps should be fairly long and the movement is usually made without running.

Remarks. – It should be noted that in practice, these movements in an "orderly fashion" require easily passable terrain and favourable circumstances. But as they have the advantage of a lesser loss of time and of a certain regularity which delays disorder, it is good to practice them. Moreover, they can be of great service on the plains, under the threat of cannon, when the marching zone is strictly limited by the neighboring troops.

2. In the approaches, when artillery fire is feared above all, the intervals between the sections should be as wide as possible; the formation of each section is of little importance. The column by two is often used because it is convenient for the march and difficult to spot from afar. The aim should be: to make the adjustment of the shot difficult and uncertain; to take precautions against prior spotting. A good way to do this is to always keep your sections at unequal heights and never have all your groups approach an accident on the ground that could serve as a landmark (ridge, hedge, road, tree line, etc.).

2. Gaining ground forward through a dangerous area

A – Concealed march of the entire company

To march the entire company over long distances through the countryside towards a predetermined objective, using all the marching routes.

The principles which should guide in the selection of formations and the conduct of the movement are as follows:

To keep one's company in hand and lose as little time as possible (which is usually not enough of a concern);

To be able to use all kinds of paths while remaining ready to expand very quickly if it is necessary to cross some dangerous passage or fight.

One will almost always march in a league of sections; a very flexible formation, easy to lead and able to mould itself in the narrowest paths (since it can present only four men abreast, the sections being in column by one) or, on the contrary, to spread out very quickly to approach dangerous passages on a front.

This flexibility – extremely useful besides – corresponds rather to the movements of the troops of second line on the battlefield (reserves, reinforcements, summer...) than to the approaches properly speaking.

B – Marching the whole company, each section on its own

account

This is the real approach march in preparation for combat and – one could say – the typical march of units in the front line in the vicinity of the enemy.

The captain indicates the objective (which may be distant and unseen), then shows the point or line of ground to be reached in the first leap; this point reached, he will give a second and so on.

He then fixes an approximate interval between the sections or indicates briefly to each section its route and designates the one with which he will walk.

If all the sections are not to leave together, he will recommend those who will have to march behind (second line or echelon) giving an approximate distance.

Finally, if the company is supposed to be surrounded, he limits on the ground the marching area assigned to it.

Each section (or marching group) is then free to move only under the following conditions:

To march on the indicated point by using the terrain and losing as little time as possible;

Do not run into neighboring sections or leave the walking area;

As soon as one has reached the line of ground fixed for the first leap, send to take the orders of the captain.

This exercise – one of the most profitable of all and one that can be varied greatly – should be repeated often over long distances through the countryside. The instructor will not lose sight of the fact that – as with all exercises in marching and using the terrain – his place is often at the sup-posed point occupied by the enemy, watching his troop come upon him; this is the best way to pick up mistakes made.

§3 – Combat

The company deployed as skirmishers having opened fire, move the chain forward

The direction of the movement is, in reality, almost impossible. Each knowing the objective to be reached and having no other concern than to gain ground in front to reach this objective, the groups advance as they can and when they can.

Also the training in view of this acute phase of the fight can only have for goal to make familiar to the men and to the officers certain very simple principles intended to guide their initiative and to ensure their solidarity.

The most important of these principles are the following two:

1. When one arrives at the decisive distance of fire (between 1,000 and 700 meters in open ground) the forward march of a fraction of the line of battle is made possible only by the fire of the stopped fractions;

2. During the entire duration of the forward movement, the fire of the stopped fractions must dominate that of the adversary in such a way as to render it ineffective (to preserve the superiority of fire).

From these principles, one can draw these practical consequences:

1. The forward march of each group must be possible without hindering the firing of the others. The chain will therefore be formed by groups that are always clearly separated, at intervals as large as possible.

The leader of a group in combat must always observe the neighboring groups. He will choose the moment when the others have opened fire to move forward.

As soon as he sees another group get up to march, he will have the firing of his guns resumed or accelerated;

2. In reality, many elements come into play to determine the superiority of fire.

We are obliged, in training, to leave aside the most important (moral factors).

The superiority of the fire, having been obtained, must be maintained during the whole time of the advance. The marching fractions do not fire; therefore, at a given moment, one can only count on the rifles of the stopped fractions. To solve the problem, it will be sufficient to advance only a certain number of groups at a time, so that the groups not marching are sufficient at each moment to ensure superiority over the enemy's fire.

Example : Let's say a line of 4 groups of 25 rifles.

If 50 rifles are sufficient to keep the superiority of the fire, we can make half of the line march at the same time (51 rifles firing, 50 marching).

If 75 rifles are needed, only one group will march at a time, the other three firing.

If 100 rifles are needed, the attack cannot advance without being reinforced.

N.B. – It is important not to exaggerate the value of such calculations, and it would be a serious mistake to believe that things will usually happen this way. The role of taking and maintaining the superiority of fire during the forward march will fall for a very important part to the artillery. In addition, it will sometimes be possible to take advantage of the depression remaining in the enemy a few moments after the cessation of a burst to make a leap all the line at once, and a well marked moral superiority will make it possible to conduct the attack with less method and more rapidity. This is what will happen most often in the last phases of the fight.

But it is essential to engrave, by frequent application, in the minds of the cadres and soldiers these two major principles of infantry combat. "One advances only by fire. Superiority of fire must be maintained during the entire period of forward movement." The habit of always subordinating forward movement to measures for achieving and retaining fire superiority is a training procedure to be recommended for this purpose.

In training, the captain may act as follows:

After the approach march, have the line which he "considers to be his first firing position occupied by a number of well-separated groups, at wide intervals, the others in support at 200-300 meters.

Have them open fire.

Superiority of fire being assumed, begin the forward movement in initially large fractions (e.g., half the groups at a time) and then smaller and smaller (as superiority is assumed to be more difficult to achieve) until one group is marching at a time.

Then continue by reinforcing.

Each group will make its leap either all at once, or (when the terrain is suitable) in small packets. These leaps, made while running, must necessarily be short.

N.B. – The short length of the jumps is necessary for several reasons. Do not lose sight of the fact that it would be much more advantageous to make them long, and that in reality they should be as long as possible.

In these exercises, which can be varied, whatever the procedures used, always require :

That a group never walks without the others pulling;

That a group walking does not hinder the shooting of the others, because then it would be better to make everyone walk at the same time;

That as soon as a group stands up, the neighboring groups accelerate the shooting.

§4 – Reinforcements. March of the Supports

The supports (front line reserves) are intended not to "push" the fighting line forward, but to supply it with men and enable it to regain superiority when it can no longer advance.

The reserve troops, until the moment they are put to the fire, must remain available – that is, in the state of coherent troops obeying their leaders – and be kept as far as possible free from loss. Getting these troops close to the battle line is a difficult problem.

Company supports (fractions not immediately deployed) may be held initially 200-300 yards from the firing line. They usually march in sections behind the gaps or better in echelon behind the wings when the terrain does not imperatively determine their place.

Each supporting section is free to use whatever routing procedures the situation calls for. Its leader is attentive both to what is happening on the chain and to the signals that the captain may make.

Knowing the direction of march, he progresses from shelter to shelter by exploiting the resources of the land. He takes advantage of every opportunity to gather his section in order to keep it as long as possible "in his hand." When it becomes impossible to shelter the supports, they must be brought to the line and made to fight.

Remarks. – We will not admit as usual the process which consists in making the support sections deployed in advance as skirmishers march behind the chain, it presents multiple disadvantages.

It is only at the last jump and to join the line of fire that the support section deploys definitively.

It can, when the terrain allows it to escape, be brought into line by small fractions.

On the arrival of a support fraction, the line of battle must resume or accelerate its fire. When this reinforced fire is supposed to have produced its effect, the forward march is resumed.

Supporters can, in some cases, intervene without joining the line of battle, especially in rough terrain where they often find firing positions to the rear or on the flanks. Their intervention in these conditions is very advantageous since they take part in the combat while remaining available.

It is good, in training, to make this practice familiar by taking advantage of all the opportunities offered by the terrain to have the supports open fire without carrying them on the chain.

Booklet 4 – Offensive Engagement of Small Infantry Units

Summary

I. Contact of the infantry in the offensive.
II. Character of the engagement combat.
III. March of a battalion vanguard.
IV. Leading company or fraction.
V. Encounter with the enemy.
VI. Summary.

Offensive Engagement of the Infantry

The explanatory statement preceding our regulation of December 3, 1904, points out as a particularity of the new combat: "The increasing difficulty, at the beginning of the engagement, to know the dispositions of the adversary, hence the more delicate, more complex and slower functioning of the contact organs."

It is useful for us to examine what, in this period of the engagement, interests the infantry officer, from the section leader to the battalion commander. It is indeed in the contact phase (vanguard or outpost combat) that the lower rank officer will most often be left to his own devices. We will only deal here with the practical conduct of small vanguards or the leading elements of large vanguards.

I – The infantry's first contact in the offensive

Before the first shots are fired (cannon or rifle), an infantry column head has only the information of the cavalry. This information, whether it comes from the fractions sent out to search for intelligence or from those who ensure close security, is summarized as follows: Such a point at such an hour is unoccupied (the most reliable negative information, in short, and the only precise one).

At such hour, received shots seeming to come from such point.

Seen troop in movement estimated at .....

These indications, which are indispensable, are insufficient to "organize" an attack and the first infantry troops have precisely the mission to remedy this uncertainty by clarifying the situation.

Their role will therefore be to sweep up as quickly as possible the enemy's still poorly determined security elements, to foil his delaying ruses, to discover and fix, as far as possible, his real front. Inaction in such a case is the worst solution; the commander of the vanguard must act energetically and without delay, the question is to know how he will be able to do it usefully.

To guide his initiative and base his conduct, the infantry commander will have, at this moment, only the following elements:

1. A mission to fulfill (a mission that must be translated at a given moment by a point on the terrain to be reached);

2. The encounter of a resistance, most often ill-defined, that will thwart this mission;

3. The terrain.

One cannot think of "setting up" an attack from scratch on the basis of these uncertain data, since the very object of this attack is still undetermined. In order to avoid long and useless trial and error, one will necessarily be led to take overall measures appropriate to the terrain, but independent of the enemy's measures, whose direction one knows only. This requires the application of a doctrine or tactic of engagement instead of following events.

One must know how to "pose."

II – Characteristics of engagement combat

In the second part of the South African war the British had given up the old methods of fighting. Marching in advance on a considerable front, when they met resistance (resistance which always had a much narrower front because of the weakness of the Boer numbers), the part of the line corresponding to the defense front was fixed at a great distance while the other fractions, continuing to march, naturally and, as it were, automatically overran it.

Many have seen this as the image of the battle of the future. The recent war in the Far East underlines their error by showing that it is still necessary today to break the enemy's resistance by direct combat. But one should not ignore the fact that direct attack – necessary and in short possible – is long and costly. The final crisis which will decide the success must be prepared by a prolonged mutual wear and tear which requires the use of numerous troops successively engaged and of powerful means of fire.

It is obvious that, when this wasted time and these sacrifices can be avoided, it must be done. Lord Roberts' overflowing non-combat engagement is unquestionably the quickest and surest way to overcome narrow-fronted resistance when sufficient numerical superiority is available.

The engagement combat of a vanguard troop will come very close to it. The British operated, in this period of the war, as if they had been pushing back outposts and recognizing a front. But as there was nothing behind the Boer detachments (quite comparable to outposts if we compare them to the English army), this first act was sufficient and there was no battle.

The engagement battle says the era of the battle in its goal and in its means. It is a question of quickly clearing the ground of isolated or accessory resistance and of determining the front of real resistance of the adversary by fixing it as far as possible, but without having the pretension to remove it. So it is a question of going fast without having the concern of economy nor of depth in order to feed a powerful attack.

In these conditions, to undertake to break by force through direct combat each point of resistance encountered would be unreasonable. One would thus play into the hands of the enemy by sacrificing time and men without utility since one can obtain the same result more quickly and at less expense.

The characteristic of our engagement combat, in front of a

resistance which appears, will be the immediate widening of the front in order to approach this "resistance" on a superior front and to overrun its wings.

Any fraction stopped in front will therefore attack – in the offensive everyone attacks – but the following fractions will immediately slide towards the wings and widen with the intention, not of reinforcing the engaged troop, but of bypassing and overrunning the obstacle.

If these first fractions are in turn caught in front, the following ones will continue the same game. The enemy line will thus be very quickly overrun and absorbed if it is narrow, recognized and, as far as possible, fixed by the combat of the engaged units if its front is wide.

The troops employed in this game of overrun can act in groups of varying strength and with varying intervals. If the groups are weak and the intervals wide, the enlargement is greater for the same number of troops, but the effort exerted in front is less. One is therefore more likely to discover the wings of the enemy front, but one is more likely to be stopped by weak curtains of posts. It is a matter of circumstances and terrain.

This method of immediate enlargement must still be the rule in the event of an encounter with another offensive vanguard. Assuming that the two adversaries have the same doctrine, the one who will take the lead in his movement will have a considerable moral and material advantage over the other.

Of course, this conception of the offensive engagement does not change anything to the usual duties of the commander of the vanguard, the one in particular to ensure his progress by occupying the points of support encountered; duty all the more strict as the uncertainty on the enemy is more complete and the distance of the bulk of the troops greater.

III – March of an advance guard battalion

As soon as the proximity of the enemy makes an encounter probable, an infantry troop forming an advance guard must renounce – whenever it is not impossible – to march in column along a road, awaiting events.

Its march will be directed towards a precise objective known to all; its itinerary will be marked out by a certain number of points on the ground (generally support points) which it proposes to occupy successively, so that at a given moment the mission of each fraction will always be: *a point on the ground to be reached.*

The battalion will not form a rigid formation moving all at once. Each company will march on its own account and in formations appropriate to the terrain towards the goal assigned to it. One of them will form the leading group, the others will march mostly parallel to each other and at more or less intervals, so as to reduce the depth, to facilitate the route and to hasten the deployment (unless the terrain or the circumstances impose other arrangements).

The battalion commander will say, for example:

"We have such and such an objective."

"Leading company, march to such and such a point (visible if. possible)."

"The main body will leave when the head has reached such and such a point, or: a few minutes after the head."

"We will first walk on such point (visible)."

Then, if he wants to march closely, the battalion commander fixes approximate intervals (intervals always sufficient to allow the captain to choose the formations best suited to the terrain) and, in the years when all the units do not march at the same height, designates which ones should follow.

If, on the other hand, he wants to take wide intervals in advance, he will give each company a particular direction or route and specify with which unit he is standing.

Whenever possible, the directions and points to be reached are "shown" on the ground.

In this way, a flexible system will be obtained, already expanded or at least easy to expand in view of a quick offensive.

There is no "premature deployment" causing delay and prejudging the dispositions of the enemy. It is a warning that is appropriate to the terrain and if one marches preferably "in width" instead of "in length," it is because one is decided in advance to widen as soon as resistance is encountered.

The greatest objection to this method comes from the difficulty of directing the movement and guiding the unit leaders.

In the present state of our morals the difficulty is serious. It is therefore necessary to change our morals.

To claim in an engagement to lead one's units like pawns on a chessboard is as dangerous as it is unreasonable. It is the ruin of any initiative and any offensive capacity.

Engagement today can only be coordinated by community of purpose, by the habit among all officers of seeing the issue in the same light and acting in the desired direction without waiting to be pushed. .

Hence the necessity:

1. To form a positive tactic. For example, in the engagement, the almost reflexive tendency to widen and to push forward in order to overrun the obstacle;

2. Never to move a unit, small or large, without everyone being aware of the direction and the goal;

3. To regulate the movements by successive jumps from one point of the ground to another in order to catch up with the other at each "step."

IV – Leading company or fraction

Let us examine the march of the leading fraction or company. And first of all, at what distance will this company march from the main body of the battalion and at what distance will it be preceded by its section or its group of scouts? This is obviously a matter of terrain and circumstances, but it is necessary to point out in this regard an all too frequent error that is very detrimental to the spirit of the offensive.

A vanguard is intended to assure to the troop that it precedes: by its distance, material security; by its engagement, the time and the information that it needs to organize its combat. Should the main body of our battalion have the pretension of making its leading company play this complete role of vanguard, and will this company, in its turn, demand the same service from its leading group? It is easy to see that this would be impracticable, and in seeking to obtain it, one wastes precious time at the same time as one removes all bite from one's offensive.

It is not in the exaggeration of safety precautions that one must seek the security of a troop on the move, but rather in marching dispositions such that this troop is always ready to fight. In an offensive march, in particular, it is too often forgotten that it is its capacity for immediate attack that constitutes the true security of a column.

The leading fraction of a company marching 300-500 meters forward can guarantee immediate surprise at short range, nothing more.

The leading company can assure the bulk of the battalion a somewhat less precarious security and give it a first indication by its engagement, but still quite incomplete and insufficient. It follows that the tin company will have to march, prepared for immediate action in the face of a surprise fire always possible and that the bulk of the battalion, although running less risk of a material surprise, will always be ready to commit itself very quickly. The best procedure to get out of trouble, at this difficult moment, is to pass without hesitation, without stopping and without waiting for further information, to an offensive decided in the form of enlargement of the front in order to overrun the obstacle.

The leading company, having received its mission in the form of the objective to be reached and, if this objective is distant, the indication of intermediate points to be successively occupied, is put on the march at a distance ahead which depends mainly on the terrain. Most often it will have to have reached the dangerous horizon or the first point of support at the time when the big one will start moving.

It will be preceded at short distance (300-500 meters) by a group (a section for example). The march of this section is regulated by its leader, who will often have the advantage of having it march in several groups, on an extended front.

The main part of the company will almost always follow in a deep formation (line of sections): at close intervals if it is completely sheltered, on the contrary quite open in open terrain. In this way, it will be possible to use the ground more completely and, in case of surprise by fire, to engage very quickly. If the intervals are wide, each section marches on its own towards the point to be reached, following the itinerary fixed for it on the ground.

V – Encountering the enemy

§1 – Leading Company

The presence of the enemy, already suspected by the reports of the cavalry, is manifested by cannon or rifle shots.

In front of the cannon, the dispositions indicated (splitting, direction known to all...) will facilitate the continuation of the movement, we will not speak of them here.

In front of the gun, one is warned only by an often distant fire whose origin is very difficult to determine immediately. One cannot, therefore, at this moment, base one's decision on the dispositions of the enemy that one does not know. Trying to obtain further information through patrols is a useless waste of time and inaction is the worst solution.

In the absence of other indications, only one decision is reasonable: to continue to carry out one's mission, which, at this point, can be summed up as a point on the ground to be reached.

When the enemy's resistance presents itself normally to the direction of the march, there is no doubt.

The leading group commits itself and tries to advance towards the obstacle. Deciding in advance to widen, in front of a resistance, to approach it on a large front, the captain only has to decide in which direction and to what extent he will widen.

As one marches in line of sections, the execution will be easy and it will suffice most of the time to slightly modify the route of the uncommitted troops, in order to direct them either to the right, or to the left, or to both sides at the same time. In the absence of orders, the section leaders will oblique themselves in the direction that seems most advantageous to them and will push forward towards the objective.

This widening, it should not be forgotten, is not intended to reinforce or extend the line of fire already formed. It must be sufficiently marked so that the groups of the wings do not cling to the same obstacle, but have chances to overrun it.

If the point of resistance is isolated, it is absorbed almost without combat and the progression continues towards the objective. If it presents a sufficient width, the wing sections, in their movement, will cling in their turn in front of new resistances that the following ones will try to overrun. If all of them collide with the enemy, we will have recognized a line equal to the front they occupy.

When the resistance manifests itself obliquely to the direction of march, the leading group, in all cases, faces and engages.

If the direction is not very serious, we will act as described above by overrunning in the direction of the march in order to reach the fixed point without losing time.

If the direction is frankly divergent and the fire is fairly heavy, the leading company will often be obliged to face it; but it will take care to extend itself without delay, when this is not impossible, in the direction of its objective in order to try to reach it at least with a fraction, especially if it is a question of an important support point.

This constant tendency towards the point of the terrain assigned as direction is the surest way to avoid being led astray and deceived by the enemy's tricks; it facilitates the leader's task.

Let us note how advantageous the march "en large" (and sometimes in echelons if danger is foreseen) is in the case where resistance is manifested outside the line of march. While the elements, marching on the dangerous side, engage, the others have only to continue their movement to extend and overflow in the direction of the objective.

§2 – The Larger Batallion

The engagement of the leading company gives a first notion, still vague and uncertain, on the situation of the enemy. According to this indication, it was necessary to act without delay.

The principle is the same: expand to overrun the recognized front.

The decision this time could be a little more mature. The battalion commander, according to the terrain and the physiognomy of the engagement, will quickly indicate his role to each company.

Remarks. – 1. It is not a question, let us repeat, of reinforcing or even prolonging the combat of the first company. The movements of the wing companies must be broad enough to ensure that they do not cling to the same obstacle and to overrun it;

2. Except in the case where he is closely followed by other troops, the battalion commander will not open his entire battalion at once and will reserve a fraction (a company for example) available at the first moment.

He must, in fact, consolidate his progress step by step by temporarily occupying the support points that are within his reach. This concern to ensure a front of resistance in case of need by the occupation of a certain number of strong points will come to the forefront in an encounter combat, as soon as the enemy will show superior forces;

3. Even in this case, immediate expansion is still the best solution. The occupied strong points must constitute as wide a front as possible, on the sole condition that one cannot invest or overrun one of them without attacking the neighbors.

Each company, moreover, – when, in its movement, it encounters a superior offensive – must not withdraw but hold on to the nearest strong point.

If the engagement of the leading company is normal to the direction followed, the battalion commander directs his "enlargement" according to his inspiration and the terrain. In the case, on the contrary, where the engagement is divergent, it will almost always be to his advantage to pursue directly and without delay the accomplishment of his mission of the moment (i.e., to reach the point that has been or that he has set for himself), by deliberately pushing his enlargement in that direction.

When, after having removed or pushed back the enemy's advanced posts, the leading battalion finds itself fully engaged in front of a front of resistance which it can no longer overrun (since it has no more available units) nor hope to remove from the front (since it has no depth), but which it fixes by the offensive effort of all its fractions trying to gain ground or which it contains, in case of inferiority, by the occupation of support points, it has fulfilled its mission.

It is now the duty of the commander of the troops to order the continuation of operations and to begin the frontal combat by bringing in, within the limits he deems appropriate, the artillery and the following battalions, while continuing the reconnaissance of the enemy's front if his wings have not yet been located.

VI - Summary

1. At the moment of the first shots, an infantry vanguard has no precise information on the enemy's dispositions or strength.

Its mission requires it to act immediately despite the uncertainty of the situation.

2. The engagement combat, intended to sweep the outposts and to overcome the accessory resistance, does not involve the frontal attack of posted troops.

Until the intervention of the artillery, the widening in order to overrun the obstacle and the investment by fire are its only means.

3. An infantry troop must never move without a precise goal. For a vanguard that penetrates the unknown (the cavalry having unmasked) this goal can only be: to reach a determined point of the terrain.

4. The danger of being surprised by fire and the decision taken in advance to expand rapidly, as soon as a resistance presents itself, oblige it to march rather in width than in depth and by autonomous fractions, to the exclusion of any tight or rigid formation.

5. Such a movement can only be regulated by marching by leaps from one point of the terrain to another; each fraction knowing its objective and determined to reach it.

6. A resistance that manifests itself and stops a fraction head-on must naturally produce the immediate enlargement of the others, with continuation of the forward movement. This habit of sliding towards the wings to overcome the obstacle must become familiar to all the officers.

30th INFANTRY REGIMENT
1st Battalion
Summary of theories

Booklet 5 – Day and Night Outposts

Contents

I – Daytime Outposts

§1 – Non-utility of a "Complete" System

A complete network of outposts as described by our field service is quite exceptional and, in a sense, theoretical. In practice the arrangements must be very simplified. Indeed :

a) The complete network, to be solid, requires considerable manpower; it is then the ruin of the troops. If one is obliged to spare the men and to enlarge the company sectors, the surveillance elements absorb everything at the expense of the resistance elements and the system is no longer solid.

b) Even if one has a lot of people, the complete network, with its continuous chain of sentries, is almost always useless. It is enough that no important detachment can pass without attacking at least one post; the range of the current weapons makes it possible to obtain this result with very wide meshes.

c) The proximity of the enemy is not a reason to deploy a complete network. It would be quite the opposite.

Faced with the imminence or at least the possibility of a powerful attack, one must seek to increase the resistance of the system. The chief's concern will therefore not be to multiply the number of small posts and sentries, but to reduce them in order to increase the strength of his Grand Guards.

The decree on the service of the armies in the field specifies the greatest freedom, and it is enough not to consider the complete system as "regular" or usual, but on the contrary as exceptional.

§2 – Partitioning

The placement of outposts may be considered as follows:

A troop on station is usually covered by companies carried in the direction of the enemy, at a suitable distance and each having an exactly defined sector.

(Note that in our detailed exercises these sectors are often too narrow; one can very well reach 1,000 meters and often more, when the terrain lends itself to it).

Each captain chose in his sector the point where he would resist in case of an enemy attack, and established the bulk of his company there. This is the Grand Guard. The line of Grand Guards constitutes the line of "outposts."

The Grand Guard itself takes the necessary security measures to avoid being surprised and to have time to defend itself (small posts of all forms guarding themselves with sentries and patrols). These are surveillance bodies and not a first line of resistance. Their mission is limited (except in special cases) to giving the time necessary for the Grand Guard to set up its defense.

(These surveillance elements will most often be provided by the cavalry during the day. Practical Instruction, art. 34).

When a large troop is stationed, it needs a lot of time to assemble and make its arrangements.

One then places between the Grand Guards and the cantonments of the main body a reserve common to several Grand Guards. This reserve often includes half of the troops assigned to the outposts (two companies out of four in a battalion).

The role of the outposts is – let us not forget – – to "resist" in case of an attack; the surveillance of the terrain is only a means of ensuring this resistance by giving oneself time to prepare it.

A leader in charge of placing outposts will therefore first ask himself: what would I do in case of an attack? how to organize my resistance? From this first decision he will deduce the way to guard himself by watching the ground. Unfortunately, we often see the opposite done and start by organizing the surveillance of the terrain and then ask ourselves, so to speak, incidentally, what we will do if we are attacked.

§3 – Observations on the Role and Placement of the Various Elements

1. Elements of resistance

Grand Guard. – We call the main body of a company of outposts the Grand Guard.

For the captain, it is important to decide before anything else the form to give to his resistance in case of an attack and the point where this resistance will be made.

In principle, he will keep as many people as possible together, the covering elements detached in front being strictly limited to what is necessary in order not to be surprised and to be able to make his combat arrangements.

It is extremely important to observe that the troops held available at the Grand Guard count alone for the resistance. The fractions detached in front are "spent." In case of an attack, after having given their own resistance, they are most often dispersed and are very likely not to reach the point where they are expected. It is therefore not necessary to mention the reinforcement that the retreat of the advanced posts could provide to the Grand Guard.

The defense project of the Grand Guard depends absolutely on the conditions in which it finds itself (terrain, strength, information on the enemy, intentions of the command, state of the troops). But this project must exist; the captain must have made his decision in advance and know what he wants to do, because he will often not have the time to "see it coming" and act according to the circumstances. This does not mean that he should not reserve the means to deal with the unexpected by keeping a reserve.

In most cases, he can be guided by the following principles:

The Grand Guard is not a reserve for the posts in front and must not bring them help.

Whenever the terrain allows for a position in the sector such that the enemy cannot pass without attacking it, it will be to the advantage of the main body of the company to carefully prepare a firm resistance, taking advantage of the power of its fire and the ease with which it can be marched due to its small number of men and the absence of smoke in its fire.

This is the best way to force the enemy to proceed with an attack in good order by keeping him in a state of indecision as to the strength and exact situation of the troop that is stopping him.

From the fact that it is advisable to keep as many people as possible on guard, it does not follow that the defense must be limited to a single point. One must not forget that the real danger is to be quickly overrun; because it is always possible with the current rifles to stop for a long time an attack even very superior.

The prepared defense should therefore always include several points leaning well on each other, so as to widen the front, and the attention of the captain should be directed to the liaison – in case of combat – with the neighboring Grand Guards. If he is on one wing of the formation, he will cover his free flank by a solid post forming an echelon in the rear.

The reserve kept available may be weak and the front of combat relatively wide, since it is only a momentary resistance. In the battle itself, one can use the long ranges and begin firing as soon as it is possible to worry the enemy; the goal is not to beat him but to make him lose his time.

From the foregoing, one should not conclude that the most advantageous form of defense would be to occupy the front one has chosen at once by deploying all one's people in such a way as to form a more or less regular line of posts, which would be very imprudent. Almost always, it will be advisable to keep the bulk of one's forces – in part available – at the point chosen as the main resistance; but one will be careful to widen one's front by occupying with relatively weak posts on one's flanks points at sufficient distance to link up with the neighboring Grand Guards and avoid overflow. The small reserve kept will be used to reinforce the defense according to the direction and intensity of the attack.

It is useless, moreover, to have the entire troop stay on the actual combat sites, and it is sufficient to be able to reach these sites very quickly (4 or 5 minutes at the most after the alert) by well-defended routes, which will be prepared if necessary.

In the case where the combat posts are at some distance from the place where the troops are staying (200-300 meters), it will be good to keep a guard of a few men, frequently relieved and well concealed. These small "trench guards" ensuring the immediate security of the Grand Guard are intended to ward off an ever-present surprise.

The commander of the Grand Guard must know in advance what he was going to do in case of an attack by a neighboring Grand Guard. In principle, and unless otherwise ordered, he should not disengage his sector, in order to rescue the troops of the neighboring sector, but he should take up arms, and if necessary, watch and reinforce the liaison with the attacked general guard, so as to prevent the enemy from overrunning his flank. This is usually the most effective help he can give.

However, if a neighboring Grand Guard is taken and an enemy column penetrates through the line, one should not hesitate, in the face of this fact, to take a vigorous offensive in the flank of this column. The need to ward off this pressing danger takes precedence, at this moment, over any other consideration.

It happens that one does not find in the sector a position such that it is impossible for the enemy to neglect the attack. If, as is often the case, a single route escapes the direct action of the general guard, a special post strong enough to resist will be placed there. (Later on, we will discuss these resistance posts, which the reserve of outposts will often provide.)

If, on the other hand, the nature of the terrain (flat and cut, wooded, etc...) and the large number of communications require it, the main body of the company will have to adopt a more active attitude. Established, ready to march, at a communications junction, it will resolutely attack the enemy columns that would have crossed the network of small posts guarding the roads.

The small posts must then be pushed further forward than in the usual case, and the careful study of communications and routes in the interim of the sector takes on a special importance.

Outpost Reserve. – The outpost reserve, having more time to orient itself in case of an alert, has more freedom of movement than the Grand Guards, and its role may not be so precisely defined in advance. However, it is essential to decide and prepare one's action in case of an alert, while reserving the means to deal with unforeseen events.

We can observe the following about this action:

The reserve of outposts must, in order to be useful, act as a whole and not spend itself in small reinforcement detachments. Moreover, reinforcing an attacked Grand Guard is a dangerous thing and it is necessary, when one intends to do so, to warn the commander of the Grand Guard in advance. There is always the risk of arriving at the moment when the Grand Guard gives way and presenting the enemy with only units on the march, poorly oriented and sometimes mixed up with the troops that are withdrawing.

Among other modes of resistance, a reserve of outposts can:

a) If the terrain in the rear of the Grand Guards presents a defensive position that is impossible for the enemy to overlook: prepare the defense of this position and rendezvous with the Grand Guards there.

b) Recognize a defensive position in the rear of each guard, which you will occupy in order to collect the company and present a new resistance.

c) Finally, to be ready to march, at a central point, with the intention of resolutely attacking any enemy column that has forced the line of the general guards.

In all cases, it is useful to place one's reserve far enough back from the Grand Guards to ensure the possibility of maneuvering (a distance of 2 kilometers, and often more, is not exaggerated for a battalion reserve).

The commander of the reserve must always let the captains of the Grand Guard companies know what he intends to do, give them a direction of retreat or a rendezvous point; finally, give his full attention to the means of communicating with them.

2. Surveillance elements: small posts, sentries, patrols

The number of troops used for surveillance must be calculated with the strictest economy. It is almost always excessive to employ half the company.

The small posts placed in front of the Grand Guard have the sole mission of giving the main body of the company time to take up arms and defend itself. It is a mistake to consider all these posts as a first line of resistance and to staff them accordingly.

When outpost cavalry is available, the small infantry posts can be entirely eliminated during the day. The entire company is then assembled at the Grand Guard.

Their strength must, in any case, be reduced when they can be equipped with rapid means of communication with the Grand Guard (cavalrymen, bicyclists, optical telegraphy, telephone).

The size of a section (50 men) for a small post is usually much too large, except in the case of special resistance posts. It can only be justified by the need to maintain three or four double sentries.

But, as we have seen, the use of a complete curtain of sentries is not to be encouraged. It is often impossible to set up and almost always unnecessary.

Isolated double sentries (200-300 meters from a post) are of no value.

Each small post (usually 10 to 25 men), depending on the size of its surveillance sector, will guard itself with a close double sentry (two at most). The connection with the neighboring posts, often impracticable and always costly, by a network of sentries, is done by patrols (insist on the necessity of patrols when one does not have horsemen).

To monitor an important point at some distance, escaping the view of the small post, we can recommend the use of a patrol (three or four men and an officer) which stays until a set time and is then replaced by another.

These frequently relieved ambushes are safer and less taxing on the men than a permanent detached post, which should be stronger.

In any case, a "small post," whatever its strength, will try to conceal its presence, to act by surprise, to deceive the enemy about its strength by a lively fire while avoiding to show itself.

Once his resistance is over, he will not allow himself to be captured but will evade the enemy by deceiving him about the direction of his retreat. It is for this reason that the immediate vicinity of a cover (wood, ravine...) is very advantageous.

The occupation of a defensive shelter (house, wall, trench...) is often recommended.

The transmission of information to the Grand Guard must be carefully planned and must be done under cover. The fact of seeing the carriers of orders or information circulate from one shelter to another is a very useful clue for enemy patrols and makes it easy to discover the location of posts.

Special posts. – When, in the sector of a company of outposts, there is a path or a communication that escapes too completely from the action of the general guard, a special post will be placed there to make a solid resistance. These posts, whose strength easily reaches one section (50 to 60 men), constitute small "Grand Guards" with a restricted sector and act in the same way.

These special posts are sometimes provided directly by the outpost reserve.

3. Establishment of outposts

Our field service contains this sentence:

"The deployment of the most advanced echelons of the security service is protected by the reserve of outposts which takes for this purpose position at the suitable point."

This very accurate prescription sometimes gives rise to strange interpretations. Without wasting time discussing them, let us just indicate how things should usually be done.

The principle to be applied is a general one:

"A troop should never be surprised."

Until it has made safe arrangements for rest, therefore, it must stand ready for battle and maintain what our fathers called "a military position."

In the case of the placement of outposts (a battalion for example): the battalion commander, having received orders from the commander of the outposts, leads his battalion in marching formation to the presumed location of its reserve. He gives (if necessary while marching) his orders to the companies of the Grand Guard, which continue, each towards its sector, covering themselves. Having chosen a position that seemed advantageous to him, the battalion commander then installed his reserve there, in a guarded halt ready to fight, until the moment when the Grand Guard companies had reached their position of resistance. This temporary location is usually in the vicinity and in front of the cantonment to be occupied by the outpost reserve.

Meanwhile, each outpost company gains its sector. The captain selects a provisional position of resistance in the vicinity of the probable location of his Grand Guard and places his main body in a guarded halt ready to fight. It is only when the surveillance elements (small posts) are placed that the company gains its definitive location and settles there.

II Night outposts

The night security service deserves a special study. It is the usual service of the infantry, because it is especially at night that the troops station and rest; moreover, the methods to be used to attack and consequently to guard during the night differ profoundly from those which we apply during the day.

All our modern infantry tactics are based on the elf of fire. Now, at night, fire counts only as a scarecrow; even at close range, its effects are materially insignificant and incapable of stopping a resolute troop. Let's see briefly how one can attack in order to deduce how one should guard.

§1 – Night Attack

Night operations are frequent but rarely involve a large attack: the risk is too great to be exposed without being forced.

Generally, they are limited to preparation: approaches, surprise removal of certain points allowing the main attack to be rushed at daybreak.

We are only talking here about these abductions of outposts.

This fact that the time no longer counts removes from the infantry all strength of resistance and restores to the shock all its value. Moreover, surprise becomes the main actor of success.

These characteristics of night combat are all to the advantage of the attack.

Two serious disadvantages compensate for this superiority:
Difficulty of conduct;
Instability of the moral balance of a troop marching at night.
The slightest ambush, sometimes even a simple stop or hesitation
can cause a panic.

A night attack can only have the aim of occupying a point of
land; its mission must be exactly defined and limited. Once this
mission has been accomplished, Elijah stops, recovers, and defends
himself. At this moment, an offensive return of the enemy is very
dangerous.

If the attack knows where it is going (exact reconnaissance of
the terrain and enemy positions) and if it is determined to go there,
it has a good chance of reaching its objective. Its strength lies in its
speed (surprise) and in the immediate threat of boarding (shock).

A troop charged with a similar mission will usually march in
groups on the roads or in the immediate vicinity. The column will
be divided into sections (sections or half-sections...) following each
other at sufficient intervals so that two of them do not fall into the
same ambush at the same time. The first pack, preceded by a few
scouts, will form the vanguard. A distance of 50 meters at night is
often sufficient.

Insist during the briefing on marching without noise and
especially on the means to be used so that each group does not lose
track of the previous one. In case of complete uncertainty, one will
walk by jumps. At each stop, one will hide one's people and send
out patrols. As soon as an enemy post is discovered, march straight
to it, disperse it, then get back in order and continue the march.

For the removal of a post, a detachment (a company for
example), if the terrain is practicable, can deploy its sections in
line in two rows, one behind the other, 30-40 meters, overrunning
each other on one of the flanks or on both, and march on it bayonet
down, without firing.

Often we will also act as we are, in column; it is especially
important to strike quickly and hard as soon as we know where to
strike.

When the vanguard falls unexpectedly into an ambush, if the
ground is free, one leaves the surprised pack to sort itself out and

passes without delay with the rest to the right or left. If you are caught in a defile, you must run into the obstacle and try to cross it.

After an effort, always gather and put your troop in order before continuing.

Whatever happens, do not lose sight of the fact that in the presence of a surprise, any hesitation, any stop constitutes the most serious danger.

It is well understood that this refers to the lead detachment, which is generally small in number (100 or 200 men) and is responsible for the coup de main.

The rest of the troop follows at such a distance that it runs no risk in case of surprise (200-500 meters).

Its role is, in the event that the leading detachment is stopped or dispersed, to immediately reconstitute another shock troop to try to turn the obstacle or break it. But its real mission is to occupy the captured point and hold it; for, if it takes few people to carry out a successful coup de main, it often takes many more to hold the conquered position.

An attack of outposts, at night, can be carried out in two ways: either by marching directly without giving the alert on the point which one wants to take, or on the contrary by making the main attack precede by a diversion on another point.

In front of an adversary who is guarding and enjoying all his means, an attempt carried out with very few people, but vigorously and noisily on a point far enough away a little before the main attack, is often advantageous.

In front of an enemy that one is likely to find numb (attack at the end of the night, bad weather, tired troops...) it is often better to go straight to the goal without giving the alert.

In summary: the attack of night outposts will be fast and brutal, very strong on its front, very weak on its flanks. Its great enemy is uncertainty; as soon as it knows positively where the enemy post to be taken is, its task is half done; very accessible to panic, any stop or hesitation resulting from a surprise can be fatal.

Finally, the most delicate part of its mission is perhaps not to take a point of the ground but to maintain itself there, because the troop dislocated by an assault, badly oriented, dispersed and nervous, is for some time at the mercy of a well conducted offensive return.

§2 – Night Defense

How then to guard oneself at night? i.e. to be ready to resist an attack of this kind.

It seems that the principles of defense can be summarized as follows:

At night, in the countryside, one defends oneself only by attacking and one attacks only by shock. From which it follows that in case of alert, at night, the first movement must be to assemble one's troop instead of deploying it as during the day.

It is necessary to avoid absolutely receiving the shock of an attacking troop head-on and to consider the ambush as the usual method of combat.

The counter-attack and the offensive return are the real weapons of defense at night. An attack by surprise or an impassable material obstacle are the only means to stop the momentum of a vigorous troop.

From these principles let us draw some practical consequences concerning night outposts.

1. Carefully conceal your posts, small or large, so as to make their discovery laborious and to prolong the uncertainty of the enemy. Place them in such a way that in no case the attacker can fall directly on them and remove them without a blow. They will therefore be placed in the immediate vicinity of the roads and paths, but outside, hidden in such a way that one can pass over them without seeing them and constituting real ambushes.

2. When approaching the enemy, in open country, when one cannot place oneself behind a serious obstacle: never deploy one's detachment across the direction of the attack; it would be infallibly taken. On the contrary, assemble it outside of this direction, hidden in the immediate vicinity, deceiving the enemy if necessary by a lively fire from a few rifles placed elsewhere, wait for the enemy column and attack it by surprise from the flank (very lively fire at close range to warn the Grand Guard and frighten the enemy, then throw yourself in with the bayonet).

If you are surprised and you have to give up the hope of stopping the assailant: in any case, give a sharp fire to warn, try to gather your people outside the direction followed, at a point designated in advance, renew your fire several times, then evade by trying to follow the enemy column. Take advantage of the first opportunity to harass the enemy in flank or tail.

3. If you have to defend a special point such as a village, a defile, a bridge - which is the usual role of the Grand Guards - never omit to barricade yourself, taking care to conceal the barricades (for example, in a village or a wood, place them a little to the rear of the edge, so that you will come upon them without seeing them and cannot avoid them. In the case of a bridge, place them at the end of the bridge on the side of the defense.) In case of an attack: the barricades will be defended by small detachments designated in advance, while the bulk of the troops will gather at a distance, at a point known to all, from which they can easily exit to counter-attack in flanking fashion the enemy column that is up against the barricade, or those that would attempt to pass to the right or left.

If one is surprised, instead of attempting a direct, disorganized and worthless resistance, try to rally one's troops at some distance at a point designated in advance and make an offensive return which, if well conducted, will often succeed. The procedure would be excellent if it were not so risky to rally one's troops at night after a surprise; it is interesting for training purposes to often exercise the troops to assemble quickly and in order.

4. A post has, at night, only a small radius of action; it can only "guard" one point of the terrain. A night outpost service cannot therefore guard or defend the entire terrain but only a certain number of selected points.

How to choose these points?

The attack can usually only march on or in the immediate vicinity of roads and paths. So we will keep the paths. But it should be observed:

That one can never be sure of keeping all the paths, especially when one arrives at night and has only incomplete maps;

That, if the terrain lends itself to it, an assailant who knows the country well can sometimes follow paths outside of communications, at least for short distances;

That finally a failure is always possible and a post, even an important one, will rarely resist a vigorous and well prepared attack.

We will conclude the following:

a) The points to be held solidly are those that the eumemi cannot neglect if he wants to make a serious attack (support points, communication nodes, defiles, etc.).

b) These points should not constitute a single line that will always be breached, regardless of its strength; other points of resistance are needed behind this line.

c) This passive occupation of certain points of the terrain never gives complete security and it is always necessary to have a solid reserve ready to march.

Let us observe that the "maneuver" at night must be very simple.

The reserve placed near a junction of roads will have the officers recognize with the greatest care, as much as possible, the routes to follow to reach the locations of the Grand Guards and the important points in the rear. In the event of an enemy attack, one will wait to be sure of the result of this attack, then one will act.

If the enemy is stopped after having occupied a point of the ground which we want to keep: offensive return led right on this point.

If the enemy has broken the line and is moving forward: take a road that cuts across the direction he is following and act as appropriate. For example: if you arrive before him, occupy a point that blocks his march and set up an ambush. If you come across it, attack vigorously. If he has passed, begin to dig in (riders if possible) and follow or wait for him.

In any case, act well together, by successive jumps, knowing exactly where you want to go each time you start walking.

This "maneuver" at night is facilitated by the use of a few horsemen.

5. It is extremely important to ensure the advantage of surprising the enemy and not being surprised by him. Surveillance must therefore be carried out with the greatest care. Let us note in this regard the following points:

(a) Every element, regardless of its situation, must ensure its own immediate safety.

b) A double sentry isolated at night at some distance from a post (100 or 200 meters) is of no value. A network of sentries is impractical. If a post is large, it can be guarded by small groups (eavesdroppers, ambushes, frequently changing patrols) hidden in dangerous directions. If it is small (6-10 men), a double sentry may be sufficient.

c) Mobile surveillance (patrols) must be very active and fill in the gaps of fixed surveillance.

d) The details of the service and the discipline are of extreme importance (service to be distributed, transmission of information, noise, light, etc.).

e) Finally, all the energy of the chief must be employed to ensure the *vigilance* of all. With tired men this is a difficult problem.

Our regulations state, in reference to small posts: "At night everyone is on watch." A leader should never ask the impossible. If he feels unable to keep exhausted men awake all night, he must take measures accordingly. It is better to have a few men on watch in the midst of their sleeping comrades than to have a whole detachment drowsy and dull.

The "watch" system is to be recommended. A rank and two or three men keep watch for an hour (or two hours at the most) and then wake up the next shift.

Remarks. – All that has just been said applies to fighting in the dark, that is to say, when one cannot use one's fire (note that the principles of fighting in the woods are similar in many respects).

It is up to each one to make the necessary modifications according to whether the night is clear or dark. In ordinary moonlight it is easier to conduct oneself, but the shooting is not much better. The moon therefore usually favors the attack; the defense must not forget this.

§3 – *Organization of a Night Security System*

It remains to indicate quickly what form a night safety system will usually take.

The division of night outposts will be the same as that which we have accepted for the day.

Grand Guard. – The Grand Guard constitutes, as for the day, the main part of the system.

Its mission will most often be to guard certain important points of the terrain (village, defile, communications node, terrain movement) chosen in such a way that an enemy attack cannot progress before having taken them.

The captain will keep the main body of his company grouped there, detaching only the elements indispensable for surveillance, and will install for defense, taking into account the principles already explained: Creation or use of material obstacles (barricades, abatis, walls, wires, etc.) defended by small guards designated in advance and having no other mission. The main body is ready at the first signal to assemble in silence on a well-sheltered point, chosen outside the main road and from which it is easy to leave to counter-attack.

If there is no point on the ground suitable for this firm resistance, the main body of the company will be kept hidden near a communications crossroads in a central position from which it can act offensively in all directions.

In all cases, it is most important that the troop be ready to assemble at the first signal, quickly and silently. It follows that the men of a Grand Guard will never be scattered, but always held together in the immediate vicinity of the point where they must assemble. At night, a troop assembled and concealed is always strong; dispersed, it is of no value.

The attention of the captain will be directed especially to the relations to be established with the small posts which must be frequently visited. He will ensure his own immediate security by means of very small groups frequently relieved, hidden at a short distance on the dangerous directions.

If the commander of the outposts does not himself designate a rendezvous point, it will be prudent to choose one far enough back and easy to recognize. Everyone should know this rendezvous and seek to reach it in case of surprise and sudden dispersion.

Outpost Reserve. – The reserve of the outposts must always be ready to maneuver at night. It will barricade its cantonment and ensure its immediate safety.

The attention of the reserve commander will be focused on the following points:

To ensure, in case of alarm, the rapid assembly of all his people, in a point from which he can easily move.

To recognize, with the greatest care, the itineraries: to be followed in order to reach the location of the Grand Guard or other important points. It will often be in his interest to have them marked out, with clearly visible objects, where one could be mistaken.

In the event of a serious attack or the removal of a major guard occupying a point of the terrain that one wishes to guard, the most advantageous mode of action will be the counter-attack if one arrives early enough, or the offensive return if the point of support has already been removed.

Knowing exactly the terrain and the point to be re-occupied, if one acts quickly and vigorously, the offensive return has the greatest chance of success.

It is prudent to designate in advance to each company of the general guard, in case of surprise or forced retreat, a rendezvous point always outside the direct path leading to the location of the reserve.

Elements of surveillance. – The Grand Guard has only one way to cover itself at night: to guard the roads by placing a post on each of them.

The location of these posts is often determined by the terrain (crossroads, bridges, defiles, etc.).

They must be far enough away from the Grand Guard to give it, in case of an alert, time to prepare; close enough, so that one can surely hear the rifle shots. Their distance can be extremely variable and it is rather advantageous that the line they form be very irregular, as this will make the mission of enemy reconnaissance more difficult.

It will often be useful to have certain points very far forward or on the flanks watched at night. Special posts of varying strength will be sent there, equipped as much as possible with a bicyclist or one or two horsemen.

The small posts, at night, do not need to be strong. Except for a mission to defend a special point, they rarely exceed 15 to 25 men and will often fall to 6 or 10 men.

When they are given fifteen to twenty-five men, it is to allow them to send out a few patrols.

A small post conceals itself; it places itself very close to the guarded road, but outside of it; if it finds an obstacle to cover itself, it takes advantage of it, but in such a way as to be able to circulate easily. It would be very dangerous at night for a small post to occupy a house, a closed courtyard, etc.)

The men stay together.

If the post is weak (8-12 men) a double sentry hidden a few steps away is enough to guard it, provided that he is well hidden. If it is stronger, it will be covered by one or two small groups of a few men (eavesdroppers, ambushes...) hidden on the paths at a short distance ahead and frequently relieved (at least every two hours).

The instruction of these small groups must be done carefully. They shoot only in case of necessity, to prevent. When one of them discovers the enemy, he warns the post, observes while hiding, and withdraws without showing himself.

The small post, if attacked, will be guided in all circumstances by this principle:

A small post is made to "warn." If it is asked to resist as well as possible, it is so that it can warn in time. Even if it is captured, if it has accurately informed the Grand Guard, its mission is fulfilled.

Therefore:

1. Avoid, by its vigilance and its ability to conceal himself, immediate surprise;

2. In all cases, and especially if there is no hope of stopping the enemy, to fire very brightly, to retreat to the point chosen in advance, and then to start firing several times.

Finally, one can designate in advance two or three reliable men to whom one gives the mission, in case of surprise, to run, without any other order, to warn the Grand Guard.

§4 - Placement of night outposts

1. The outposts being placed during the day, switch to night service.

No difficulty. The captain instructed each rank in advance of the arrangements to be made for the night, according to the instructions of the commander of the outposts. The movement was made at the moment when it was no longer possible to see clearly enough to fire.

The only important point is to conceal this movement and the locations chosen for the night.

The Grand Guard remained under arms during the movement of the posts.

N.B. – An attack at nightfall, which presents multiple disadvantages for the assailant, rarely occurs.

2. To place outposts when arriving at night on the ground.

The orders being given according to the map, the main difficulty is to reach without error the location that one must occupy and to orientate oneself there exactly. Therefore, for the reserve of outposts and for the Grand Guards, one should always choose points that are easy to reach and that one can recognize without error (crossroads, hamlet, bridge, etc.).

In order to orientate each echelon, it is advisable to lead the entire battalion to the location of the reserve. The Grand Guard companies will leave from there, accompanied by a reserve officer who will thus know the exact location of the Grand Guard and the path to follow, and will gain the point they must occupy. They will be installed there as it was said, taking care to put themselves immediately in defense (barricades if it is necessary, recognition of the immediate surroundings). We will push a few meters ahead of the posts to cover it.

Do not neglect any precaution so that everyone knows where to face, where the neighboring posts are and where the paths we are guarding lead. This is not always easy.

3. Change from night duty to day duty.

Even in the case where one only has to take back the places left the day before, the operation must be done with precaution. Daylight is the most advantageous time for an attack and one should not be surprised while on the move.

In addition, it is extremely important - especially for the Grand

Guard - to take up, as soon as one can see clearly enough to fire, a position that will allow him to use his fire.

If, therefore, we do not have to set out at dawn, it is necessary that the Grand Guard take – even if only for an hour – a position allowing good resistance to the fire. The surveillance will be more active in the last hours of the night, the patrols more frequent and pushed further.

In any case, one hour before daylight, the weapons will be taken up and the commander of the Grand Guard will watch for the moment to make his new arrangements (it is good to have taken up the daytime posts as soon as one can distinguish a man at a hundred meters).

The small posts will be moved, if necessary, only when the Grand Guard is installed in its "day" position.

N.B. – If one has arrived on the field at night, the commander of the main guard will take advantage of the first light to choose a provisional position of resistance which he will have the main body of his company occupy while he proceeds rapidly with the reconnaissance.

About the Author

Louis Loyzeau de Grandmaison (1861-1915) was a French military theorist and staff officer. One of the key proponents of what would become known as the Cult of the Offensive, his writing and teaching provided part of the groundwork for French military doctrine heading into the Great War. He was killed in 1915 while leading the Fifth Army Reserve Group.

www.ingramcontent.com/pod-product-compliance
Lightning Source LLC
Chambersburg PA
CBHW072141090426
42739CB00013B/3242